Madelein

" Add ventu
moment you

Enjoy the book.

Antonw

Moving Mountains

Andrew Townsend

Antonw
26/1/22

Published in the UK by Wide Blue Yonder Media

Source ISBN: 9781916886513
Ebook ISBN: 9781916886506

Moving Mountains: Running from the Atlantic
Ocean to the Mediterranean Sea.

1. Andrew Townsend 2. Ultra-Runner 3. Travel
4. Adventure 5. Trail Runner

www.andrewtownsend.com

Off to the mountains I go to lose my mind and find my soul.
(after John Muir)

To Judy, Louise and my family

Prologue

I arrived in my mid-fifties, clinically obese, riddled with arthritis and often having to walk with a stick.

I had an epiphany, threw away my stick and resolved to change my life for ever. I started walking every day. The walking turned to running and after two years I had lost a third of my body weight and was fitter than I had been since my twenties. I started running all over Europe and pushed myself harder and harder. In 2015 I ran eight self-supported marathons in eight countries in eight days driving myself between each one - a world's first. As I approached my sixtieth birthday, I wanted to mark it in a really spectacular way. I decided to emulate the world's greatest trail runner, Kilian Jornet, and run across Spain from the Atlantic to the Mediterranean. The journey would take me 525 miles across the Pyrenees climbing a total of more than 125,000 feet – the equivalent of four 'Everests'.

This is my story.

CONTENTS

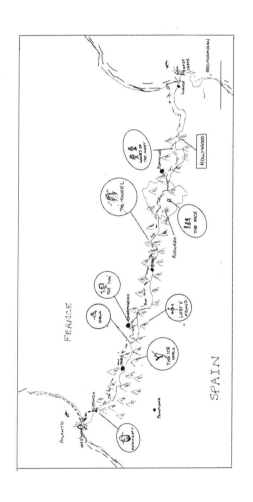

Chapter 1

An idea is born …

"You have to go after happiness in life, you have to look for it and find the things we love the things that make us feel alive. Life isn't something to be preserved or protected. It's to be explored and lived to the full."

Kilian Jornet

It was 6.00am on a cold and wet Sunday morning and I was lying on the sofa, Mimi the spaniel snoring contentedly on my lap. In my other hand was a cup of coffee and perched precariously on the back of the sofa was my iPad logged into YouTube.

Sundays nearly always started like this, particularly cold, wet October ones. I was summoning up the energy to go on my long run and was watching a few inspirational videos to help me brave the elements and pass the time before dawn broke. Little did I know that I was about to see something that would change my life for ever.

I loved watching the great runners hitting the trails - Sage Canaday, Rickey Gates, Courtney Doulwater and, my favourite, Kilian Jornet. He had everything - speed, agility, grace and what's more he came across as being truly humble despite excelling in his sport. A real adventurer, someone to aspire to even though he had 30 years on me - but a boy can dream - right!

I really should get going I thought, but the sofa was inviting, it was very wet outside and besides Mimi looked so comfortable - one more video! This looked interesting "Kilian's Quest - Pyrenees - Part 1". Well after I watched "Part 1" I watched "Part 2" and then "Part 3" and then I watched the whole thing again - I was transfixed. How could someone do that, run 500 miles, climb more than 40,000 metres and do it in just nine days - unbelievable!

I finally made my way to my 'playground', the Thames

Path, and started running. As I splashed through the puddles my mind kept returning to the Pyrenees and the incredible images I had seen in Kilian's video. I don't know whether it was the landscape, the imposing mountains and endless waterfalls, or if it was just the sheer scale of the adventure but from that moment I was 'in'. When I finally returned home wet and bedraggled several hours later, I fired up my iPad and found a map of the Pyrenees. I opened a drawing programme and drew a wavy line across the Pyrenees from the Atlantic to the Med and posted the picture on Twitter with the caption "and for my next trick". Now I was committed!

Over the coming months, particularly on the cold, wet days, my mind returned to the Pyrenees and, yes, I watched the video again and again. Little did I know that it would be another 20 months before my dream became a reality and I would be on the plane to Bilbao.

In the meantime, I kept piling on the miles, mostly along the Thames Path interspersed with a monthly trip to Europe. With a friend, I had decided to run a marathon a month for 12 months in 12 different countries. The trips were distinctly lacking in 'planning' and involved a quick scan of google earth to find 12 different countries, some

lakes or mountains and preferably a photogenic city to in-
corporate on the trip too. I had already run through
Bruges, done a marathon in three countries in one day
(not as difficult as it sounds with Holland, Germany and
Belgium all meeting at Aachen) and ran through the vine-
yards of Moet et Chandon. November came and another
country - this time an ultra-marathon through the streets
of Vienna and the bitter cold of the Danube. I had already
run an ultra in the summer, the iconic 100 km "Race to
The Stones" and that, and the Viennese adventure, had
given me increased confidence that I was comfortable
with the extra distance.

Then, the following month, in December 2014 and on the
spur of the moment I decided to tackle 'The Beast of
Provence', Mont Ventoux. If the name rings a bell it's
probably because it is one of the most well-known Tour
de France stages, the mountain where the Tour de France
rider Bobby Simpson lost his life, and the stage that truly
sorts out the men from the boys. It's also recognised as
one of the windiest places in the world with wind speeds
recorded in excess of 320km per hour and is certainly not
designed to be run up - it sounded ideal!

So, on boxing day I set off on the long drive down to

Provence and the little village of Bedoin which represents the start. On the drive down I felt terrible. I had a cough, sore throat, felt weak and was having trouble breathing - this was not a good sign. If I have any physical attributes in life suited to distance running, it is strong legs and a fantastic respiratory system and with any of these failing the challenge was going to be even more difficult. However, I was also blessed with a steely determination (or perhaps just a low IQ) and I wasn't going to let this set-back de-rail the adventure. I had a day to prepare myself and then I was ready for the off. As so often happens with me, the weather changed, the wind dropped, the rain was replaced with sunshine and a beautiful day lay ahead. I won't go into the details of the run here (or perhaps I should say stagger and crawl) but suffice it to say that somehow, after seven hours and as the sun was setting, I found myself on the way down from the summit and heading towards the warmth and comfort of Bedoin.

On reflection, this run and indeed all the runs and training before and after, was leading me inexorably to the Pyrenees. I had found hidden depths that I didn't know I had. I had not only braved the elements but had done so when I was feeling at an all-time low (it later transpired that I had a severe respiratory infection which was sorted out with a course of antibiotics and a month lay-off).

I finished the 12-marathon challenge by the summer of 2015 and by October I was starting to get restless again. I hadn't forgotten about the Pyrenees and the amazing video I had seen but it seemed such a daunting prospect and the few people I had mentioned it to thought I was mad. But if I had learnt one thing in life it was that people's default setting was 'no' and I was definitely a 'yes' man - in the nicest sense. Still, I decided to lower my sights temporarily and set myself a different challenge. I had really enjoyed my European adventure, the thrill of discovering new places, meeting new people and of course the running. But I had visited 12 countries already, what could I do that was new and inspiring, both to me and the people who were following my journey?

I trawled the internet for ideas - multiple marathons, ultra ultra distances, exotic locations, it had all been done. What I needed was a challenge that would exemplify all my attributes and skills - an appalling lack of planning, the inability to say "no" and a total disregard for self-preservation. Then in hit me - seven marathons in seven countries in seven days; what a challenge that would be. Multiple country marathons had been done before of course, even seven consecutive marathons in seven continents, but this was going to be entirely self-supported and what's more I was going to drive myself between each country.

The dye was cast, and I started 'planning'. I devised a route that would involve running eight marathons in eight days in eight countries. I would start in Berlin and end in Venice taking in Prague, Vienna, Bratislava, Budapest, Zagreb and Ljubljana en route. With a friend, I would run a self-supported marathon in each country and then hop in the car and drive to the next destination. Simple - what could possibly go wrong? Well, I write about that particular adventure elsewhere but suffice it to say that I somehow completed the challenge despite numerous speeding tickets, getting stopped at borders and my friend getting injured during the third marathon, necessitating me completing the other five 'toute seule'. As I finished the final marathon on day eight in Venice, tired but elated, one thing was clear to me, the Pyrenees adventure was 'on' - I could do it.

As soon as I returned home, I started planning in earnest. The first decision was to work out whether I was going to camp on the trail or try and find places to stay at the end of each day. I really wanted to travel 'light' and stick as close as possible to Kilian's quest although I wouldn't have the luxury of having the Salomon Team behind me, carrying all my stuff and sorting out my accommodation. No, the decision was made I was going to pack everything I needed into a running rucksack and take my chances on finding somewhere to stay at the end of the day.

Next job was to decide on the route. For most of my adventures I relied on Google Maps, but I would have to take this a bit more seriously. I emailed Salomon and they gave me a rough guide to Kilian's route starting at the lighthouse at Cap Higier on the Atlantic coast and finishing at the Cap de Creus lighthouse on the Mediterranean. From his stopping off points (there were only eight) I could work out a rough route. It looked like he was following a mixture of the famous 'La Senda' trail and the 'Haut Pyrenees' route.

Preparations were moving on at a pace - I had rung round to a few newspapers, radio stations, equipment manufacturers and, true to form, no one was interested in me or my trip. I was used to this response from the eight marathon, eight countries attempt but it still puzzled me when on the rare occasions I did listen to the news or read the papers I was aghast at the banality of some of the content. Never mind, a solo trip it was to be. I had great fun selecting a suitable rucksack, a fine balance between finding something that I could actually fit more than a pair of socks into and something that I could lift off the ground - after all I was meant to be running.

The final step was to book a flight to Bilbao, the first night's accommodation in Irun and to try and find my passport.

No turning back now - I was on my way.

Chapter 2

Up, up and away …

"Adventure starts the moment I leave my door"
Gloria Steinem

On reflection I should have tested my brand new Solomon rucksack before I was leaving - or at least packed it anyway. I was horrified at the weight; how on earth was I going to lug this the 525 miles across the Pyrenees? (Subsequently I did weigh the pack on some rather 'kind' home scales and it came in at 7.5 kg). I unpacked everything for the umpteenth time and looked for something I could discard. My eyes lit upon a stick deodorant and I substituted this for a mini-ature bottle of essential oil - well the cows wouldn't mind I reasoned. I also discarded one pair of knickers, a T-shirt and a pair of socks - total weight saving at least 100g.

I slept fitfully and I had already been sitting outside the house patiently waiting for the taxi that was to take me to the airport for at least half an hour before it arrived. I checked and re-checked my passport and credit cards and clutching my *Guide to the GR11 Trail* which had arrived the day before I waved goodbye to Judy, my ever-supportive wife and hopped into the taxi and the start of my great adventure.

As the plane swooped over the Pyrenees on its approach to Bilbao, the sun glistening on the snowy capped peaks, I felt a sinking feeling in the pit of my stomach. What on earth was I thinking and just what was I trying to prove? I was 60 years old for heaven's sake and society dictated that I was past it (whatever 'it' was) and I should be confining my sporting activities to a little jog around the park. But there was another part of my nature that had started to emerge since the eight marathon challenge that said, "you've worked hard all your life, you deserve this, have fun and embrace the unknown". The last emotion was particularly alien to me. Whilst I had always had a reckless streak, I was also a creature of habit - I had to sit in the same place near a door, I couldn't cope with crowds, I watched the same films and read the same books again and again. Was this really the same person who was about to launch himself into the unknown.

Anyway, I didn't have time to reflect further as I found the bus that was to take me to San Sebastián where I would catch a train to Irun and the foothills of the Pyrenees.

The station at San Sebastián was spectacular with an enormous high glass ceiling and beautiful mosaic paving. This was a reminder that the adventure was not just about the run but also about the sights, sounds and people that I would meet on my travels - "keep your eyes and mind open Andrew" I repeated to myself.

Before long I had dumped my bag at the hotel and was trotting through the streets towards the lighthouse at Cap d'Higier which was the exact spot that Kilian Jornet had started his trip a few years earlier. I was determined to follow his route as closely as possible although it would probably take me longer than the nine days that he took to cover the 500+ miles!

It hadn't taken me long to change into my running gear though, because after all that was all I had with me. My one nod to propriety was a pair of over-trousers in case it rained and hopefully I wouldn't have too much use for them. This really was a new departure for me as I normally packed the kitchen sink when I went anywhere from a range of computers to several jerseys, coats and shoes to cover all eventualities. As I jogged along the bay I went through my inventory - two pairs of shorts, Hoka running shoes, one pair each of leggings and over-trousers, a few running tops, T-shirts, a running jacket, a rolled-up puffer jacket, socks and knickers. That covered the clothes, next the toiletries; a toothbrush, a small tube of toothpaste and a miniature bottle of lemon essential oil. And finally sundries - a mobile phone and charger, a wallet, a small notebook and pen, my Suunto watch to track the mileage and elevation and two 500 ml water bottles. This was the sum total of my worldly belongings.

I skirted round the side of the lighthouse and there it was, the Atlantic in all its glory. Of course I had to stick my paw in, after all this was the official start line, before trotting back to the hotel where I could change into my party clothes, aka a clean T-shirt. I found a nice restaurant where I could sit outside and watch the world go by whilst eating some delicious tapas. I've no idea what it was as the menu was in Basque but I sensed that keeping to a remotely vegan/vegetarian diet on this trip would be quite a challenge.

It was a good feeling to sit there outside the restaurant watching families and friends enjoying themselves, talking animatedly, on a warm balmy evening punctuated with laughter and the noise of happy children playing. I wanted to tell everyone about the adventure I was about to embark on and for them to share my excitement but there would be time for that later.

I headed back to the hotel and bed - it had been a long day. My last sight before drifting off to sleep was of my rucksack perched on the hotel chair winking at me ….

Chapter 3

The adventure begins …

" And into the mountains I go to lose my mind and find my soul"
After John Muir

I was packed and ready for the off at 6:30am. I ran down to the beach to shoot a quick video where I was greeted with a glorious sunrise, surely a good omen for the trip. Next to the lighthouse again for the start and the obligatory pictures and I was on my way, it really was happening.

It was probably after about mile two that two thoughts

came to me simultaneously - firstly, I couldn't believe
how heavy the pack was, but on the positive side it wasn't
swinging round too much and I had at least got
everything in …. The second thought was a vision of my
iPhone charger hanging out of the wall in the hotel room.
"Bugger". I retraced my steps and somewhat sheepishly
retrieved the charger from the room and set off again. I
could sense what the receptionist was thinking - "if he
can't even leave the hotel room how on earth is he going
to get to the Mediterranean".

Anyway after my false start I was on the road again and
trotting towards the outskirts of Irun where I would pick
up the GR11 trail proper. As I approached the last
scattered houses and shops my eyes lit upon a little café.
"Well a five-minute stop for a coffee wouldn't hurt and
besides the caffeine would be good for me" I reasoned. A
quarter of an hour later I was wiping up the last of the
crumbs from the muffin and struggling with my rucksack
- the time had come to start this adventure.

I found the GR11 without too much trouble (the red and
white flash markings will be indelibly printed on my
mind for ever) and started the long climb out of the town.
First impressions - very hilly (surprise, surprise) and hot,

already the temperature was in the high 20s. The views were absolutely breathtaking, the slate and stone path winding its way through green rolling hills and fields and all the while getting steeper and steeper. Irun was by now a speck in the distance, a mere dot barely visible on the shores of the Atlantic. I passed a sleepy farmhouse perched on the side of the hill and for a while I shared the broad path with some goats who didn't seem particularly interested in me, despite the sight of a hot, sweaty, thirsty sexagenarian ponderously making his way up the steep path. I was sure I was getting to the top as I wended my way through a wood with sunlight streaming through the leafy trees. It was here that I had my first encounter with the Pyrenean cattle that were to become such a familiar sight on my adventure.

Now before we go too much further it's probably time for me to come clean about something … this manly, intrepid adventurer has a fear of cows - they don't even have to be bulls; cows, calves, heifers, they all have the same effect. But this trip was all about facing my fears so coming to a region with one of the highest concentration of cattle in Europe was a good place to start. But I digress, the path was broad, the wood was extensive and my heart was strong and the cows and I managed to keep a respectful distance from each other.

I was now getting really thirsty. I was only able to carry one litre of water in two 500ml bottles and with the heat and the incline those had long ago been emptied. But as was to happen so often on this trip, my prayers were answered, and I came across a stream with a little water-fall. I stripped to the waist and gave myself a good dows-ing before slaking my thirst and filling my bottles. I wasn't sure what the protocol was about drinking from streams but this one looked clean and was flowing fast and besides I was thirsty. Little did I know that as the trip unfolded and the heat became more intense I would be-come less and less picky about choosing a water source. Next, food - the last thing I had eaten was a banana four hours previously but I hadn't seen a single soul since I had left Irun so the chances of a café or shop were slight.

The sun was beating down but I kept going, conscious that this was just day one and I still had some miles to go before I arrived at my destination, Bera. I had run out of water again and the tell tale signs of dehydration were kicking in, dry throat, headache, etc. I was heading up the side of a valley and hundreds of feet below me I could see the glinting of a stream but I wasn't going to risk

leaving the track and scrambling through the undergrowth. I could hear the buzz of chain saws in the woods
so I knew there were people about, although I couldn't
see them. Finally, I reached the top of the track which
came out onto a road that crossed the dam. As I trotted
across the head of the dam, I looked longingly at the millions of gallons of water to my right but it was completely inaccessible - water would have to wait.

Then as I rounded a bend, I saw an ancient chapel surrounded by a picket fence. Maybe, just maybe, I would
find my own salvation in the form of water. I slipped
through the metal gate and down the path to the chapel
entrance and there on my right was a water tap. I
couldn't believe my luck this must be water from the dam
for thirsty churchgoers and mad runners too. I drank and
drank, remembering to take some salt tablets, and filled
my bottles - this should be enough to get me to the end of
the stage.

I was elated as I skipped up the path, it was amazing how
such a small thing as a sip of water could make such a
difference to one's demeanour; there was a lesson hidden
there somewhere. Now all I needed was a nice restaurant
and something to eat I chuckled to myself. Well they do

19

say that the Lord moves in mysterious ways so you can imagine my absolute amazement when I saw a sign 'Cafe Olaberri – 300 m'. But the chances of it being open were minimal, I hadn't seen a single soul since leaving Irun, just a few goats and cattle and the sound of the woodsmen in the distance.

It was worth the risk, after all what was an extra 600 m in the scope of things. I wended my way up to the cafe and sure enough the car park was empty and it looked deserted but I tried the door anyway. Yes! It was open and as I made my way to the bar a bright, cheerful lady appeared from the back. I could tell she was somewhat taken aback by my appearance, but we both put a brave face on it, as if a hot sticky man dressed in skimpy shorts and a T-shirt and covered in dust was an everyday appearance. My new friend didn't speak much English but we managed to establish with various mooing and baaing noises and depictions of horns that I didn't eat meat. She smiled and disappeared into the back again before re-appearing a few minutes later with an enormous baguette and half a kilo of cheese - delicious. Next something to drink - I settled on two cups of coffee and three little bottles of a drink called Aquarius (little did I know that this was to become my secret weapon in the battle to cross the Pyrenees and I would consume hundreds of litres of the stuff over the coming days). Finally for pudding I settled on a Kit Kat. I took my ill-gotten gains outside and sat at a little table in the sunshine gorging myself and thinking that life couldn't get much better than this. All aches and pains forgotten.

As I was trying to summon up the energy to gird my loins, I heard a whooping and hollering and at that moment, a peloton of aspiring Tour de France riders arrived. All different shapes and sizes but wearing the obligatory lycra and brightly coloured shirts - what a sight for sore eyes. They piled into the café and into a back room that had been laid out for them. So this is why the café was open, my good fortune again.

I made my way back to the road and after a few metres re-joined the GR11 to take me to Bera and my destination for the night. I only stopped once to lie down under a tree, my head on my pack soaking up the late afternoon sunshine. This was really living. No time to reflect too deeply though as I still had a few miles to go and so it was with a spring in my step that I crossed the bridge into Bera. I found a little shop where I gulped down a two litre bottle of Aquarius much to the alarm of the lady serving in the shop and wolfed down a large packet of peanuts.

I found my hotel and there to my amazement were the 'Tour de France' team drinking cold beers under the brightly coloured sun umbrellas, chatting animatedly about their day's exploits. They seemed pleased (and amazed in equal quantities) to see me. I'm not sure that was exactly the same sentiment of the lady who owned the hotel as I presented myself at reception to check in. But she was lovely and friendly like the vast majority of people I met on my adventure and she gave me a wonder-ful room with a balcony overlooking the garden.

Now I've already told you that I was travelling light so before I could relax I had to do my washing. I stripped off my clothes and put them in the base of the shower be-fore joining them and pummelling them with my feet. All I needed now was to start singing and I would be like the African ladies from my childhood doing their washing on the rocks by the stream. I hung my clothes and myself out to dry on the balcony and sat at a little table writing up my notes and watching the sun fade behind the moun-tains.

I took stock of the day - Cows +1, Snakes 0, Getting lost +1/2, Water -1, Food -1, happiness +10. I had run, walked, staggered just over 23 miles and climbed a total of 3,000 feet - not too bad for day one and just another 500 miles to go. Kilian at this stage would have been about 35 miles ahead of me but there was still plenty of time to catch him.

I can't remember what I had to eat but it was delicious and I do know that I was asleep as my head touched the pillow dreaming of cows, bikes and adventures to come ....

Chapter 4

Running in the clouds ...

"The secret of happiness is freedom. The secret of freedom is courage"
Thucydides

I woke with a start. Where was I, what time was it, where did I have to be? And then I realised, for one of the few times in my life, it didn't matter and perhaps it never did. Was this what freedom felt like? Whilst I lay on the bed pondering this, I did a quick body check. I felt a bit stiff, but no blisters and no pains in the joints either. I'd eaten well last night and made sure I'd drunk plenty of water too. In fact I felt really good and ready to go.

I showered, proudly gathered up my clean laundry which had dried to a crisp and proceeded to re-pack my rucksack. I gave it a cursory lift ... no it hadn't got any lighter during the night - damn. After a quick breakfast of rolls, jam and coffee and having waved goodbye to the patron I was on my way.

I gingerly made my way past the sleeping 'Tour de France' bikes and navigated to the edge of the village and the familiar red and white markings of the GR11. I had only run about two kilometres but already the stiffness was starting to dissipate - this was going to be a breeze ... wasn't it?

Although it felt humid there was a thick mist and low-lying cloud as my pace slowed to a crawl in harmony with the ever-steepening path. I passed a field to my left where there were a few goats also stretching and welcoming in the day. But these weren't ordinary goats. For some reason they had decided to perch on top of the flat roof of the goat shed instead of inside it. Just time for a couple of photos of this extraordinary sight before continuing the long laborious trek up the path.

For the first time I had trouble picking up the markings of the path as it became less defined with the lack of use. Before I had set out, one of my many fears was of getting lost. I was reckless enough to do this alone but not quite stupid enough to not realise that the mountains could be dangerous and that the weather could change in a heartbeat. Because of space limitations I really was stripped down to the bone and not prepared for a prolonged stay on the mountain. My mind was wandering again and I had lost the markers. I backtracked down a little way before I saw the familiar red and white chevrons painted on a stone and I was on my way again ever upwards. "Concentrate boy, pull yourself together, you've still got 500 miles to go." This was not to be the only conversation I would have with myself over the coming weeks … after all who else was there to listen to me.

Gradually the cloud and mist started to thin and I arrived at the top and into bright sunshine to be greeted by a sight that took my breath away. There below me was a thick blanket of cloud with just the tops of the trees and the peaks breaking through as far as the eye could see. I took a few pictures before pressing on along a ridge and through a sparsely wooded copse before arriving at a newly mown hayfield with an old farmhouse and an even older tractor perched in the corner. It was getting really hot now and the cloud had long ago lifted as I crossed onto a small single-track road which, to my amazement, led to an enormous café, one woman, one dog and one cup of tea. I was right on the Spain/France border here and, luckily for me, the cafe was where the border post would have been. No food but I was sure that I would find something later ... wouldn't I? I took my tea and her dog and I sat out in the bright sunshine thinking that, once again, ain't life grand.

There is a saying amongst ultra runners "beware the chair" - in other words never sit down because the temptation not to get up is too great. I was aware of this as I reluctantly put on my pack, gave the dog a final pat and continued my way up the track which before too long became a path again. Another long climb, one of several that day. But things were looking good. I hadn't been able to run as much as I thought I would and progress had been slow but the scenery was breathtaking and although I was hungry the water was holding out

Now it's as good a time as any to give you a brief life

history on the importance of hydration to runners. Well, it's absolutely vital - you can't survive without water for very long and some very interesting things start happening to your body if you get severely dehydrated including, but not limited to, headaches, dizziness, nausea and even kidney failure. The tell-tale signs are dry mouth, headache and dark coloured pee. I must admit that these important facts weren't uppermost in my mind when I skipped into a farm yard with a water point some ten miles from Elizondo, my destination for that evening. The superb 'Guide to the GR11' did mark the water points but of course these changed with the seasons and they weren't always easy to find, so the golden rule was "a bird in the hand" …

The rusty old tap was right in the corner of the cobbled farmyard which was fine but the downside was that it was guarded by two ferocious, snarling dogs on chains. A quick bit of Pythagoras and I calculated that the chains were just long enough to put my left buttock in serious peril from the dogs' jaws. I still had a little bit of water in my flasks and although it was really warm, I decided to plough on.

An hour later and I was regretting my decision not to

have braved the dogs. There was no sign of the sun abating and I had squeezed every last drop out of the bottles. I sat under a tree to rest and get my bearings. I wasn't that far from Elizondo now and there was no point in feeling sorry for myself, I would just have to plough on. Fifteen minutes later I was perched on the edge of a trough which was had a little pipe feeding water into it. It had happened again; the gods were well and truly on my side. There was even a bright red cup that had been provided for thirsty travellers.

So it was with high spirits that I skipped into Elizondo, a sprawling farming village, nestled in the mountains and made my way to the one and only bar I could find. I proceeded to have my, by now, customary three cans of Aquarius supplemented with a litre of water and a cup of coffee before my eyes alighted on the plates of tapas that were sitting forlornly on the top of the bar with the odd tired fly buzzing around. The charming barman spoke good English so it was easy to identify and hoover up the vegetarian tapas - there was an omelette, some potatoes and something else which I didn't enquire too deeply about. Anyway I was replete ... for the moment and started chatting to the barman. He was fascinated and amazed at what I was trying to do and I think slightly disbelieving that I was serious. After all I was less than 50 miles from the start. He told me that Kilian had indeed come through the village on his epic trip but when they all rushed out of the bar to cheer him on he had already gone - he was that quick. Hmm they won't have that problem with me I mused as I picked up my rucksack, said my goodbyes to the barman and set off to find the hotel on the edge of the village.

The hotel was simple but had a really nice atmosphere. There were some locals talking and laughing and sipping from cold bottles of beer whilst their children played happily on the patio which was covered by a huge awning to protect them from the sun.

I got to my room, stripped and prepared to do my washing although I really didn't feel like it. As I was about to step into the shower I caught sight of myself in the bathroom mirror. Peering through the dirt and sweat streaked face and framed by matted hair were these bright burning eyes with a twinkle in them that I hadn't seen for a very long time - Yep, I was going to be alright.

This was a family hotel in the true sense of the word. I was the only guest but wasn't lonely as the family joined me at my table as I ate my supper. The children did their homework occasionally glancing up at me to try and work out the who, what, why.

Although the locals were still partying outside it was a hot night so I slept with the shutters open and before long I was dreaming about goats perched on roofs, shangri-laesque mountains appearing through the clouds and waterfalls ….

Chapter 5

Meetings and greetings …

"To live is the rarest thing in the world. Most people exist that is all."
Oscar Wilde

S o what had brought me to this quiet, remote village in the foothills of the Pyrenees from the hustle and bustle of the city? What was I running from?

In truth, I think I was always an adventurer and wanderer at heart. I was born and brought up in a remote part of Tanzania, East Africa where my father was a District

Commissioner with responsibility for the welfare of the Masai. My mother was pretty intrepid too - she was born in Australia and had studied medicine at Adelaide University. Her first trip out of her home town, Adelaide, was to hop on a boat and travel 7,000 miles across the ocean to do her PhD in London, but not before stopping off in East Africa to visit a friend. On arriving in Mombasa she travelled by train alone to the heart of Tanzania where she not only met her friend, but my father too and three months later they were married.

My childhood was idyllic and like something out of a 'Boys Own' annual. My earliest memory is sitting on a tartan blanket underneath the jacaranda tree in the garden in Monduli eating birthday cake with Mum and Dad. In truth every day was like this - chocolate cake days. In the morning my Mum would pop me outside under the tree with just a hat on and nothing else. I was guarded by our black Labrador, Tess, and I would often fall asleep nuzzled up on her tummy. I was taken everywhere on safari, I played in deserted streams with natural water slides carved out of the rocks over hundreds of years, I ate around a flickering camp fire surrounded by laughter and chatter, I caught snakes with a fork stick, I made catapults, I slept under the stars in Masai bomas and I never felt safer or happier.

So was this where it all started, this yearning for adventure? Time to reflect more on that later. Back to the job in hand. Today was going to be different. My brother and sister-in-law were on holiday in Spain and had agreed to stop off for a few days en route to their destination to catch up with me.

I had breakfast with the hotelier's family and reflected that, regardless of location or nationality, we were all very much the same. Late for school, homework not finished, missing shoes and breakfast grabbed on the run.

It was so comfortable and homely here and the family had been so welcoming, but I knew I had to press on and I donned my rucksack (if that's the right expression) - anyway whatever the correct terminology is, it hadn't got any lighter. I didn't bother with any stretches, after all if Kilian didn't why should I, and I trotted off to find the path and maybe even the great man himself. As I found the familiar red and white chevrons I noticed a man get out of a car in full running gear. This was unusual in itself. I hadn't seen a single other runner since I had left Irun, but even more extraordinary was that he was the splitting image of Kilian, same lithe figure same curly dark hair. Anyway we said our "buenos dias" to each other as I went on my way and he got ready for his run. The path was already getting steep and I was slowing to a crawl when suddenly there was a rush of wind as 'Kilian' sped past me skipping over the rocks like a chamois. "It's only because he isn't carrying a pack" I said to myself as I soldiered on.

As I toiled up the path I saw a figure ahead walking at a steady pace with a large blue rucksack that looked even heavier than mine. As I drew up alongside we exchanged greetings and I walked with him for a bit. He was a student called Pascale and was spending a fortnight hiking along the GR11 before returning to university. He was somewhat aghast at what I was trying to do but just at that moment our conversation was interrupted by a figure flying down the mountain at full tilt. It was 'Kilian' who had obviously got to the top and was now coming back and returning to his car. "He runs a bit like me" I explained to Pascale "although he's running a bit on his heels". "Sure" said Pascale trying to keep the smile from his face. We wished each other well and I pressed on towards a hunter's lodge which I knew had a water point.

As I arrived at the lodge I was amazed to see three ladies in full hiking gear complete with expensive looking boots and poles. I had barely seen a soul on the trail for the first few days and now I had met five people in one morning - this was like Piccadilly Circus. I introduced myself to the Spanish ladies and after a bit of toing and froing we settled on French as our means of communication. They were on holiday and were having a few days out in the mountains. They proudly told me that they were all in their seventies and had been doing this for years. I told them what I was up to, but they didn't seem particularly impressed and the most forbidding of the trio was looking me up and down, weighing me up. "You speak French just like my son-in-law" she announced. "Thank you", I replied swelling with pride. "He's English, has a terrible accent and I can't understand a word he says either".

At that moment Pascale arrived to save the day. The ladies departed and a few minutes later I was on my way too. I could hear the ladies chattering animatedly and laughing up ahead, but strange as it may sound, I felt like being alone again. I veered off the path and headed straight up the mountain, cutting the corners off the zig-zagging path and soon the voices faded into the distance and I was left only with my thoughts for company.

Thirty minutes later I was at the top and I took a few minutes to catch my breath and take in the panorama. Mountains and valleys fading into the distance as far as the eye could see, a sight that I would never tire of over the coming weeks.

But, breathtaking as the view was, I didn't linger for long as I knew I had to try and hook up with my brother and his wife at a refuge in the valley before another long climb and my stop-off for the night. A quick check to be absolutely certain that there were no vestiges of food in my pack (there weren't) and I was off. The sound of the babbling stream soon replaced that of my grumbling tummy as I descended through an enchanted wood. The path making its way through the trees and the lichen covered stones and boulders. This really was like being in one of those magical fantasy films and I had a bit part to play. Down and down I went skipping from path to boulder and sometimes leaping across the stream - for the first time on the trip I felt like a proper trail runner, this was what I had come for.

As I reached the valley floor the path got wider, the

stream bigger and there in the distance at the end of the track I caught the familiar sight of my brother's car parked outside Kinto Cottage. "Hi, great to see you … have you got anything to eat". As I wiped the crumbs from my mouth after my fourth flapjack I looked earnestly at the map with Nick, whilst pretending it meant something to me. All I knew was that I had to keep going east and eventually I would hit the Mediterranean.

I waved goodbye to Nick and Gill and the flapjacks and started the ascent. I ran until I was out of their line of view and slipped into a rhythmic walk - gosh I was tired.

I was running along the Spanish/French border and had to keep a close eye on the markings as this is where the GR11 meets the GR12 (the French equivalent). There were even tales of the French hopping over the border and moving the markings to disorientate the travellers - surely not. I also had to keep one eye on the horses and cows who were sharing the hillside with me but we managed to keep a respectful distance from each other.

With a sense of direction like mine, I have studied the anatomy of getting lost at length. It starts with a nagging feeling at the back of your mind that something is not quite right. The next stage is to increase your speed (often in the wrong direction) before the deep thud of realisation that you are hopelessly lost. The perceived wisdom is to re-trace your steps until you find a familiar landmark where you can get your bearings and re-join the correct route. But not me, I knew better. I was pretty sure that I had picked up the wrong path and was actually on the French side so rather than re-trace my steps I decided to head across the scrub on the top of the mountain and re-join the path at the bottom again. After all no point in doing three sides of the triangle - right?

I ran like a madman along the wide ridge of the mountain through the brush and rocks making a b-line for where I thought I would be able to make the descent. Sure enough as I got to the edge of the ridge I could see the broad, white logging track snaking through the trees several hundred feet below. There was no path, but I took my bearings and started my descent crashing through the shrub and undergrowth before coming to an abrupt halt at the edge of what appeared to be a sandstone cliff. From the top I hadn't been able to see this at all. It was a natural haha albeit a very steep one. My heart sunk, the logging track was so near yet so far, just a few hundred metres away. The cliff stretched for 100 metres in either direction and it was flanked by thick, impenetrable under-growth. I could re-trace my way back up the mountain through the shrub or ….

It's amazing one's attitude to risk and how it changes as your comfort zone is expanded and pushed ever out-wards. Already on this trip I had started to see life differ-ently and that the risk and danger was all part of the ex-perience. After all if you considered the facts, a direction-ally challenged man in his sixties with no food and little water alone in the depths of the Pyrenees you would probably re-evaluate your life too.

The decision was made - I was going to slide and slither down the sandstone cliff face. It wasn't shear and it would be akin to sliding down a steep ski slope which I had done several times before. Also I had watched count-less videos of Kilian do it. What could possibly go wrong?

I took a deep breath and launched myself off the edge. It was actually great fun until I was near the bottom and caught a root with my foot which launched me head first into a bush. "Well that's one way of stopping" I thought to myself as I picked myself up and did a quick check.

Nothing torn or damaged, the pack was in one piece and so was I. With a broad grin, I made my way onto the logging track and ever eastwards.

Things got even better when after a few kilometres I met a couple of woodsmen who assured me I was on the right track for Burguete and I would be there within the hour. I was feeling pretty pleased with myself as I trotted along the track. I had got lost and found myself again, I had glissaded down a sandstone cliff and I was only an hour away from a shower and some hot food. In fact I was feeling so pleased with myself that I decided to take a short cut across an enormous field - after all no point in doing three sides of the triangle - right?

Half an hour later I was still in the field, surrounded by horses and an impenetrable fence. I was furious with myself, would I never learn. But as stubborn as ever I refused to go back and ended up crossing over a stream and getting wet feet before re-joining the track where I could see the tail lights of my ever patient brother's car.

I slumped into the back of the car exhausted but elated Despite getting well and truly lost I had somehow managed to find my way down the mountain without having to re-trace my steps and get to the rendezvous, albeit 45 minutes late.

As a treat, we had booked a nice hotel in Eugi, due south of Burguete on the shores of the lake. My brother would bring me back to the start point in the morning. After a shower and a bit of 'Masai washing' of the clothes I donned a clean T-shirt and decided to put on my running over-trousers to add a bit of sartorial elegance to the hotel restaurant clientele. The three of us talked animatedly over supper as I caught up on the news from home but before long I could feel my eyelids getting heavy and I was aware I still had to write my notes and get ready for the morning.

As I lay in bed I took stock of exactly where I was geographically. I opened up a map of the Pyrenees on my phone and put a digital pin down to mark where I had got to. I still had a long, long way to go but I could see a bit of land between the sea and the pin - I was making progress. I had run about 65 miles and ascended more than 12,000 feet and I was only about 10 miles behind schedule. I could make that up somewhere … couldn't I?

I awoke several hours later with the light on and still

clutching the phone. Tomorrow was another day.

Chapter 6

Communing with the cows ...

"The greatest pleasure in life is doing what others say you cannot do."

Anon

After a hearty breakfast of rolls, jam and coffee I was dropped off at the previous days finishing point ready to start the next leg. It was a slightly later start than I wanted but I was glad of the extra rest. Although I had a hard day ahead (what day wasn't), I was confident that I would make good progress because I had the luxury of a lighter pack as I was returning to the same hotel tonight.

Remembering my mantra from San Sebastian (gosh that seemed an age ago) of enjoying the journey and keeping my eyes open I had found out a little about Burguete. I knew that the Irati river ran through it and that Ernest Hemingway had described it in his novel *The Sun Also Rises*. In fact Hemingway had lodged here during the twenties. Now there was someone who really did his own thing - would I see his ghost on the trail I mused as I left the outskirts of the town.

The path was wide and relatively flat and I made quick progress through the woods before descending down a steep path leading to a very old church which seemed to be situated in the middle of nowhere. They must have been very earnest worshippers way back then although there were lots of youngsters milling around laughing, joking and sharing their picnics by the side of a little pond. Idyllic I thought, although in the back of my mind there was this little voice that kept on repeating "what goes down must go up" and how true that proved to be.

Now you will remember from day one my confession about being fearful of cows. Well the first few days had passed without too much incident, on the cow front anyway. When I did come across them, there was a state of armed neutrality where I would be able to make a small detour thus allowing both parties to save face. But inevitably there came a time when I had to front up. I had been climbing for a couple of hours and had passed field after field before following a narrow track which contoured along the side of the hill with a barbed wire fence one side and a heavy thicket and a very steep drop the other.

I rounded a bend and there my worst fears were realised, perhaps 10 – 15 cows with calves milling around a long water trough and blocking the path. I weighed up my options – to walk through them … I don't think so! To turn back and try and find another path further up … a non-starter, I was already tired and I just couldn't afford the time to tag another three or four miles on to what was already going to be a long day. The thicket to the right of the path was dense and that coupled with a very steep drop left me with no alternative but to climb over the barbed wire fence and try and find a way through the brush and brambles and then re-join the track when I was safely past them.

The cows stared at me in disbelief as I perched precariously on top of the barb wire fence and launched myself into the brambles the other side. I slid along the fence feeling my legs and arms being caressed by the thorns and nettles, but I finally found myself, grazed and battered, a few feet past the cows with a potential crossing point back on to the path using the side of the water trough. I took a leap of faith and somehow found my footing on the side of the water trough, one foot went in but I found purchase with the other and jumped onto the path in one seamless movement, running as fast as I could away from the somewhat startled cows. After 50 metres I turned back to see that the cows hadn't moved an inch but I still like to think that I brightened their day and that they will remember the fence jumping, bramble negotiating, trough walker who came to visit them that day.

As for me? Well that was just one of my many encounters with the cows on that trip; but by the end, whether through tiredness or familiarity, we both accepted each other and I was allowed as a visitor to their paths and fields!

I didn't have long to congratulate myself as by now it had started to rain and it was time to put the wet weather gear on for the first time in earnest. I use the term 'wet weather gear' loosely as this consisted of a wafer-thin pair of running bottoms (fresh from their sojourn in the posh restaurant) that seemed to get wetter the longer you wore them and my faithful Salomon jacket.

By now I had left the cows and the fields long behind and I was scrambling up a really steep path towards the top of the ridge. The path gave way to a boulder field and it was getting increasingly hard to find the familiar GR11 chevrons through the mist and rain. I finally got to the top and ran along the ridge with thick shrubbery on one side and a shear drop on the other - now was not the time to slip I thought to myself. Then a momentary lapse in concentration had allowed me to veer off the ridge and I realised I was lost … again. I scrambled up through the thicket and eventually found the ridge and the markings again.

For the first time on the trip I felt thoroughly demoralised and I wondered whether this was really going to be beyond me. I sat on a boulder and with rain dripping off my cap and trickling down the back of my neck I took stock. I was cold, wet and hungry. I had had the run in with the cows which had unnerved me and I was covered in cuts and grazes. My gear was clearly not up to the job and I hadn't even got to the snow fields yet. When the markings and the visibility were so poor one had to concentrate like mad and yes it was dangerous, one slip and I could be lost for days up here.

As I sat there on the boulder my despair and self pity turned to shame and I gave myself a metaphorical slap in the face. I was having the adventure of a lifetime and I was doing something that I loved. I was free, away from all the constraints and hustle and bustle of everyday life and I was in some of the most spectacular scenery anywhere in the world. I was fit and injury free and yes I was a bit uncomfortable but this was all part of the journey and what's more I bet you Kilian wouldn't be moaning about a bit of rain. And I remembered his words "You have to go after happiness in life, you have to look for it and find the things we love the things that make us feel alive. Life isn't something to be preserved or protected. It's to be explored and lived to the full."

I felt invigorated and donning my rucksack I got off again with renewed purpose. I left the route markings to my right as I sped off into the cloud and drizzle on the wrong path. It was a good half hour before I realised I was completely lost. But the lecture to myself had done me some good and I knew it was downhill to the finish point and besides it had stopped raining. I dug my phone out of the rucksack and prayed for a signal and a bit of battery. My prayers were answered and taking a bearing on where I was trying to get to, I climbed over a barbed wire fence and scampered down the hill.

The problem was that directly in line with where I was trying to get to were a series of obstacles ranging from enormous rock walls to shear drops, to barbed wire fences. But I pressed on skirting around the rocks and drops climbing over the fences until finally I reached the valley floor. I hadn't been able to get a signal for a while but I now saw that I was way below the designated finish point. However I worked out that if I could stay on the logging track I should eventually find my way home and what's more it might still be daylight.

By now I had less than a couple of miles to go but there was one final obstacle in my path. The track had led to an enormous pair of metal gates and a compound that was guarded by two dogs. The fence was completely secure but I could see a possible way round it. It would mean climbing up a steep escarpment (what's new) which they hadn't bothered to fence, skirting along a ridge and then I hoped I would be able to find a way down when I was beyond the property and the dogs.

I set off spurred on by the thought of a hot shower and something to eat. Forty five minutes later, covered in a new set of cuts and bruises, I was atop the ridge looking down onto the farm below and my destination, the track the other side, probably less than 500 metres from where I had cut up the mountain.

Never mind, no time to dawdle as I rejoined the track and after another mile saw the familiar and welcome sight of my brother's car. I had made it after 10 bruising hours and 5,000 feet of ascent and more importantly 22 miles closer to the Mediterranean. I hadn't seen the ghost of Earnest Hemingway but I had learnt an important lesson that no matter how bleak things looked to remain positive and I would somehow find my way metaphorically as well as physically. Little did I know how useful this lesson was to become in the days and miles ahead

As we poured over the maps that evening, me nodding

sagely making out that I understood the paths, contours and strange symbols, we got some disturbing news from the Patron. The roads to today's finishing point and the start of tomorrows stage were going to be closed for a huge mountain bike race. Even if I could somehow get to the start the paths would be completely taken over by mountain bikes.

What was I to do? I just couldn't afford a lay day - I had to press on if I was going to meet my goal of effecting the crossing in 21 days. I bet you Kilian didn't have these problems I mused. But as usual my ever resourceful brother came up with a plan. We were moving hotels further East anyway so I would simply do the stages out of order. It meant a two-hour drive for Nick and Gill but they were happy'ish to do it if it kept the show on the road. I was very grateful for their generosity but in the back of my mind even my rudimentary map skills told me that a late start and a long day weren't perfect bed fellows. There was also a nagging feeling that this was a self-supported adventure and that I was cheating in some way. But then I reasoned that Kilian had had the support of the whole of the Salomon Team, including meteorologists, strategists, nutritionists as well as his inspirational mother, Naria. He had lifts to and from the night stops, massages to relieve his aches and pains and pacers to accompany him.

"Cheating bastard!" I thought as my eyes closed and my head touched the pillow simultaneously.

Chapter 7

Lost and found …

"Only those who will risk going too far can possibly find out how far they can go."
T.S Elliot

The drive to the start of the next stage, the romantically named Zamia Parking, was long but was enlivened by my brother's commentary on the effectiveness of the EU road funding programme. I won't trouble you with the details but I sensed he thought that the money could have been spent more wisely than on these enormous carriageways solely occupied by us.

It was 10.30 when I finally waved them off with the details of where we were to meet that evening ringing in my ears. I knew that there was no time to dawdle as there was several hours of hard running and climbing ahead of me if I was to get to the rendezvous before the light went. Now with the best part of 100 miles completed and over 20,000 feet in the bag you may be wondering how my body was holding up. Before I set off I had so many pre-conceptions about how I would fare health wise, from blisters to broken bones and my continual back problem from a slipped disc that I had got 18 months earlier. But I can honestly say that I felt fantastic. The stiffness that had been present on days two and three was not so per-sistent; yes I was permanently hungry but for the most part the water was plentiful which was just as well as I was only able to carry one litre in two 500 cl soft contain-ers. I was amazed too at how my feet seemed to be hold-ing up as I had suffered from blisters and lost toenails in the past.

So it was with a spring in my step that I set off up the wide, gently inclining dirt track, flanked by the river be-low me. I glanced down and noticed a camper van parked next to the river. "What a fantastic spot to camp" I thought to myself as I drew parallel to the van. At that moment a man appeared from the side of the van and gave an enormous stretch. Nothing unusual in that you might think except that he was completely naked. He glanced up at me and gave me a hearty wave … at least that's what I think it was. With great English reserve I waved back sheepishly and feeling somewhat inadequate, put my head down and made my way to the end of the track which petered out into a narrow mountain path.

The climb wasn't too bad and it wasn't long before the camper van was a small white mark on the meandering river bank below. I couldn't put my finger on it but I felt uneasy today and as I climbed I tried to find a reason. Since I spent so much time on my own, with just the mountains and the rivers for company, I had developed a knack of being able to get in touch with myself. Sift the thoughts in my mind - a type of 'mental panning' if you like and get to the root of what was playing with me. Very new age'ish although I smiled at my attempts at meditation and mindfulness at home. Sitting in a half lotus position on my yoga mat trying to empty my mind whilst at the same frantically counting down the minutes when I judged that enough time had elapsed and I could respectfully finish my meditation and escape outside. My attempts at mindfulness had been similar - raking the leaves in a slap dash way so I could escape for a run to the river.

After maybe half an hour I had found the answer. I knew that with the late start and the long drive I was going to be really pushed to finish the section before nightfall and even if I could get in touch with Nick and Gill there wasn't really an accessible escape route. No, I would have to finish this one way or the other and, with the Prezl head torch lying on my desk back in England, it would have to be in the light. As I sat on a boulder catching my breath I had one further thought. I was so grateful for the support of my family but in a strange way this had taken away some of my independence and purpose - a paradox really and probably a lesson in life somewhere. How reliant we become on other people for our purpose, safety and wellbeing.

Anyway enough philosophising for the time being, I had a job to do and as if to reinforce that I saw two figures running and power hiking up the mountain behind me. I recognised the 'nudist' although he had some shorts on and with him was his very attractive girlfriend also with clothes on. I set off again trying to run although it was too steep for me and I slipped into a power hike before the couple caught me up. They both spoke perfect English (as usual I was ashamed by the sparsity of my language skills) and we established that they were here on holiday enjoying the beautiful mountains. They asked me where I was going. "Cap de Creus" I said as casually as I could. "But that's on the Mediterranean, where is your gear?". "This is it" I sheepishly replied. "Well the snow is lying low this year so I wish you good luck - here take this" and with that they handed me their bottle of water before shaking my hand and heading off down the mountain.

I was amazed at people's generosity on this trip not just in material terms but with their generosity of spirit. In England my lofty ambitions would have been greeted with a sucking through the teeth and a dozen reasons why I would be wasting my time and never complete the journey. Here it was very different.

I kept looking at my watch like the mad hatter in *Alice and Wonderland* and every time I did, I tried to go faster and faster. But I had now reached a boulder field which I had to pick my way through carefully and inevitably this slowed me down. Another glance at the watch and another rush forward but I still seemed as far away from the summit as ever and one of three things struck me; One - my watch was wrong, giving me the wrong distances, two the GR11 guide and the maps were wrong, three I had miscalculated. I wondered to myself which was the most likely. I scrambled up a scree slope and finally I had reached the summit of Chipeta Alto. I looked 360 degrees around me, the master of all I surveyed - although of course there is only one master in the mountains and it certainly wasn't me. The scene was spectacular with the Pyrenees stretched out in front of me as far as the eye could see, snow-capped peaks, water cascades and valleys with winding rivers. This Shangrila was there just for me. I had always been a bit of a loner so I loved the solitude but the vastness of the panorama did make me feel very small and insignificant, like a pin in the desert, which on reflection was probably not a bad thing.

Tick tock, tick tock a quick slug of water and it was time to move on and start the long descent into the valley. I knew I would be able to make some time up here; the path was well defined and I wouldn't have to concentrate so much on keeping to the route. I set off whooping and hollering like a wild banshee careering down the mountain at what felt like breakneck speed - I was really getting the hang of this, Kilian would be proud of me. At precisely the moment that the old adage "pride comes before a fall" came into my head, my foot skidded on a patch of loose gravel and I was dumped unceremoniously on my bum. The force knocked the wind out of me and my first thought was how lucky was that I hadn't gone head first but instead landed on the part of me that had the most padding. I sat there for a minute getting my wind back and gingerly taking stock. A bit of a graze, almost certainly a nice bruise ahead and a bit of a dead leg but otherwise no lasting damage. I had been lucky and not for the first time I recognised how totally alone I was - not a soul for miles around.

I continued my descent, a bit more carefully this time before I finally arrived at La Mina and a crossroads of paths and decision time. At major way points the GR11 often has some helpful information signs in addition to the red and white chevrons. Typically these will give a distance and approximate time (based on a fast walk) to the next logical stopping point. These varied in accuracy but depending on the terrain and elevation I could always knock some time off on the basis that I was running not walking. So it was with some dismay that I realised that however I chose to interpret the signs I was going to be really pushed to get back to habitation by nightfall. But what choices did I have? I could return from whence I came and phone my brother with my tail between my legs or press on and hope for the best.

By now you've probably got to know me a bit and you will understand that going back wasn't an option for me. So after a sip of water and the last of the fruit that I had 'borrowed' from the hotel's breakfast table I set off at a canter up the wide path towards the rendezvous point some 13 miles and 3,200 feet away. The wide path soon gave way to a track and that in turn gave way to yet another boulder field for me to scramble up. As so often the struggle was worth it as, when I approached the top of the boulder field, I arrived at the opening of an enormous lush emerald green hanging valley with a river winding through it surrounded by the ever present snow capped mountains and cascading waterfalls. I stood and not for the first time on this trip I gawped open mouthed - what a stupendous sight.

I set off at a jaunty pace - the path was well marked, the terrain was flat and I could concentrate on running and more importantly making up time. I wended my way along the valley, occasionally crossing a zigzagging stream towards the foot of the mountains. The cloud was starting to thicken on the mountain top but I knew that all I had to do was make the ascent and then head down towards the rendezvous at Andach where a shower, a bed and a warm meal awaited me (and not necessarily in that order either). The path led me to a final stream to cross before rejoining it the other side and into the mountains. I even managed to cross the stream without getting my feet wet - things were going my way.

The path was steep but I kept going singing all the ultra runners mantras to myself "one foot in front of the other", "pain is inevitable suffering is optional" and my favourite "it's mind over matter - if you don't mind it don't matter". In fact this is only one of the diversion tactics that ultra runners use. They vary from counting to 100 and starting again and again (a la Paula Radcliffe). A bit like counting sheep but more painful. Or Rachid El Morabity, the famous Marathon de Sable runner who runs for 15 minutes then has a sip of water and then starts again for the next 15 minutes on the basis that anyone can run for 15 minutes. My personal favourite is to take a deep philosophical question and ponder on it. Like "Does the study of philosophy ever lead to answers or just more questions?" or "does crime pay - a study of the UK banking system". But actually in these surroundings all I needed to do was look around me and marvel at the nature; I wanted to savour every moment and not miss a thing.

I was bought out of my reverie with a bump. I had been climbing and climbing and as I got higher a thick fog had descended and I realised, not for the first time, I had lost the way markers. Hopefully the way I have described the journey thus far, has given you an idea of the beauty and majesty of the mountains but the fact was you had to concentrate the whole time. It was all too easy to miss a marker and the paths were so steep in some places it would be quite possible to just walk off the edge into the ravine. My mind was whirring and now I was fully focussed. I was already tight for time and I felt I was close to the top so re-tracing my steps, although probably the wisest choice, was discounted. I got out my phone and prayed for a signal (I hadn't had one for several hours but you never know). My prayers were answered and I navigated to Google maps. There was the little blue pulsing dot that marked my position and nothing but empty space around. I expanded the map and I could see where I was heading for. I edged forward and the dot moved ... in the right direction. So I decided to keep going in as straight a line as I could and when I started the descent and the fog cleared I would, signal permitting, take another reading and pick up some landmarks.

By now the terrain was interspersed with areas of compacted snow that was stubbornly clinging on to the last vestiges of winter so I knew that I was approaching the summit. Sure enough, minutes later, I reached the top and, as I had predicted, when I started the descent the fog lifted. Out came the phone - yess! I still had a signal and I took some very rough bearings on the rendezvous point. The light was beginning to fade as was the signal so now I was on my own with just the memory of the map imprinted on my brain. I ran down and down by the side of fast flowing streams, waterfalls and a hanging lake shrouded in mist. It was beautiful, eerie and I felt as if I wasn't alone but on and on I went, climbing over fences scrambling over rocks but always going down and straight. I was exhausted and, with no way of contacting my brother, was starting to look at rocks that I could take shelter under. But there in the gloom was a sign, the first one I had seen for several hours, and I was back on track with just a couple of kilometres to the car park and safety. The relief was palpable but I still had to get to the bottom down a narrow, rocky and steep path in the dark. Finally I burst through the bushes into the car park. I could see a car at the end with the engine running and the lights on - it had to be Nick and Gill, I had made it. As I approached the car wondering what the reception would be like the car revved up and I was left running despairingly after the retreating tail lights shouting "it's me, it's me come back".

I sat on a rock with my head in my hands and took stock - I had run over 22 miles and climbed more than 6,000 feet, had fallen, got lost and was covered in scratches and bruises. I hadn't eaten anything except the fruit I had 'borrowed' from the hotel and I had run out of water. But something miraculous was happening; rather than sit there feeling sorry for myself as I would have done a few days ago, I looked for a solution to my dilemma. If there was a car park there was a road and if there was a road there would be cars or at least the road would lead somewhere. I heaved on my rucksack, exited the car park onto the road and started walking up the hill towards Andach. Before long my phone was squealing excitedly with a myriad of missed calls and texts. I had a signal and it wasn't long before I was sitting in the back of the Golf on the way to the hostel. Nick and Gill were very gentle and understanding in the circumstances but I knew I had caused them a lot of anxiety and for that I was truly sorry.

But more philosophising on that later. It was time to recover and find something to eat.

We arrived at our pit stop for the night, Andach. A typical small ski resort with a hotel, a few shops and a pizzeria although it was bereft of any snow so not at its most attractive. I was deposited outside the large hostel while they drove onto the hotel with a rendezvous arranged at the pizzeria for 8.00pm.

The hostel was enormous and very 'concrete', a bit like a modern hospital. It was also deserted. I finally found the reception desk where there was note asking me to phone a number. Gosh this was like a Harry Potter adventure. I duly phoned the number and as soon as I got the "hola" I asked in my best French "do you speak French?". "No, I'm Spanish" she announced in broken English "you missing traveller, I come".

Sure enough ten minutes later, a small, neat and energetic lady arrived through the doors. I gave her a huge smile and she gave me a huge beaming smile back. A smile is a universal language and I knew from that moment that we were going to be alright. If she was startled by my dishevelled appearance she never once let on. "Where is

your sleeping bag?" I smiled blankly, "towel?"…
no "sheets" … no. "Wait" … she scuttled off into the
back and re-appeared with a towel and a pillow case. We
smiled at each other again and she led me to my room.
The room was small with two bunk beds around the walls
and a tiny bathroom off it. I found some blankets in a
cupboard and a pillow and 'made my bed' choosing one
of the top bunks. You may wonder, with all my aches and
pains, why I wanted to do yet more clambering but I had
a fear of confined spaces and just felt safer …. Although
on reflection the ceiling was quite close!

The room was warm and the water hot and I just stood
under the shower watching the colour of the water swirl-
ing down the plug hole turn from dark brown to beige to
clear. I felt so much better and the aches started to evap-
orate as I did my 'African washing' and draped my
clothes over the radiator to dry. Time to break out the
glad rags and go and party. I found a cleanish T-shirt and
put on my over trousers - a bit muddy but they would do.
On with the clean socks and wet running shoes, which
were showing worrying signs of wear, and I was ready
for action.

I wandered down to the Pizzeria and Nick and Gill were

already there at the table waiting for me. We ordered the biggest pizza we could find and a huge beer. I knew what was coming but they were too kind and gentle to make a big deal out of it. Me getting lost had put them under a great deal of stress and my brother, who was an experienced mountaineer, emphasised how dangerous the mountains could be. I hated confrontation but in my heart I knew they were right - I was spectacularly badly prepared. I could barely read a map, let alone use a compass (not that I had either). My gear was not up to spending a night on the mountain and the phone signal was erratic to say the least.

But I also knew that I had never felt more alive in my life and that somehow I felt protected and that I would complete this journey safely. Deluded, self centred, selfish - all of those things but maybe this is what would carry me through to the end.

As I headed back to the hostel, comfortably replete, I reflected on the day and all the cliches presented themselves one after another. Yes I had been lucky, but I was still in the game. Fortune favours the brave. Think about the here and now. Don't live in the past. And finally, as I turned the key in the lock, was this really the same timid, self-conscious, people-pleasing and insecure person that had left England a fortnight ago?

Chapter 8

The waterfall …

"Enjoy yourself, it's later than you think."
Chinese proverb

Today I was doubling back to complete the stage that I had been forced to leapfrog. It looked a much easier day on paper, about 21 miles with 4,000 feet of elevation. But I was already learning to prepare for the unexpected. I loved the excitement (although not always at the time) and the challenge of overcoming obstacles, but endurance running is as fatiguing mentally as it is physically and part of me longed for an 'easy' day. I wanted to be able to marvel at the landscape without the constant nagging feeling of was I lost, would I make the rendezvous point on time?

And this is how it was. The path was wide and relatively flat and I was able to make quick time. The track was obviously used by the lumberjacks as there was an avenue of neatly chopped and stacked timber lining the route. Needless to say it was completely deserted and I had the whole valley and mountains to myself with the exception of two mating lizards joined 'end to end' - "that's novel" I thought as I took a picture.

What was also novel was not being lost and I had every chance of making the rendezvous in Zamia Parking on time. I was running well too - there was an incline (wasn't there always) but I was able to maintain a steady, albeit, slow pace. I had experienced this sensation before, an almost zen like feeling, with the only company the sound of your breathing and the rhythmic pitter patter of your feet on the track. Breathe in, breathe out, breathe in, breathe out, pitter patter, pitter patter and ever eastwards. Suddenly there was huge commotion from the side of the track as two wild boars squealed loudly running off into the undergrowth – my first sighting of these famous Pyrenean inhabitants.

I was making good time but, after the debacle the day before, I was clock-watching, determined to make the rendezvous on time. It was so strange to be out here in the middle of nowhere, without a soul for miles around yet to still be ruled by the clock. Something to ponder on maybe for my next 'philosophy' session - "*the past and future have no power over you. Only the present—and even that can be minimised*" - discuss.

I awoke from my reverie to the sound of water in the distance and as I rounded a bend in the path there before me was a beautiful waterfall with the mountain water tumbling into a crystal-clear pool. As a rebellion against my earlier thoughts on 'time' I took my shoes and socks off and sat on the edge of the pool dangling my feet in the water. It was heaven. With my thirst slaked and full water bottles I carried on with renewed energy. I wasn't even phased when I saw a discarded snake skin in the middle of the path - time for that later.

I came to a fork in the path and in synergy with the rest of the day decided to take the easier 'road' route, although in reality it was a narrow single track with passing places. I climbed over the hill, moving casily, and skipped down the path alongside the road to the rendezvous at Zamia. There was even a small café at the bottom

surrounded by motorbikes selling ice cold lemonade -
perfect.

My brother was in seventh heaven too and not just with
the surroundings either. A car had managed to get its
wheels over the edge of the slope and Nick, using all his
ingenuity and civil engineering skills, was working out
how to retrieve it. Needless to say the operation was a
success and it wasn't long before the grateful driver and
his young family were on their way.

We drove back to the hotel chatting happily and arranged
to meet in the pizza café for supper. I wasn't as tired as
usual but then I had only done 21 miles and climbed
4,000 feet - hey perhaps I was getting used to this and
had uncovered Kilian's secret. (Little did I know what
was in store for me over the coming days).

As a solitary person I had always been very observant of
my surroundings and in particular observant of people. If
something or someone didn't quite fit I was onto it immediately (not that it ever served me in any way), but I think
I would have made a good spy albeit without the booze,
broads and guns. As we approached the café I noticed a
man outside smoking. Nothing unusual in that you might

think but there was something about him that just didn't quite fit. We were high in the mountains surrounded by mountain people - rugged, weather beaten, uncomplicated even. The smoking man was the antithesis of this. He was slender, wearing expensive loafers with tassels and no socks and sported a rather tired pinstripe blue shirt hanging out of his jeans. He was in his sixties, unshaven with long greyish hair swept back a bit a la Johnny Holiday. That was it! He looked a bit like a faded French film star, you know the type - chain smoking Gauloises and always with a drink in his hand.

Anyway he gave us a cursory nod as we entered the café and ordered food, food and more food. We had a happy evening and I continued to observe the man in between mouthfuls of pizza. He was obviously the 'Grand Fromage' of the village as he had his own seat in the corner, didn't appear to buy a drink and everyone seemed to defer to him. I decided to nick name him 'The Don'.

Chapter 9

Traversing the ice wall …

"The true courage is in facing danger when you are afraid"

Frank Baum

Sometimes you just have one of those days.

I awoke feeling tired and out of sorts and with a sense of foreboding. I'd had a quiet, uneventful day yesterday in the grand scheme of things and today looked to be fairly straightforward, albeit with a steep climb. Perhaps I was missing the sense of danger and excitement that I had experienced earlier in the expedition. I

caught myself - how on earth could I take these wonderful mountains for granted, I was so lucky to be here and I
should revel in every moment. There was another voice
that also reminded me that I should be careful what I
wished for. If I wanted excitement and danger then these
mountains were the place to find them.

It was early but I knew the café would be open and I
would be able to grab something to eat before I set off. I
didn't want to disturb Nick and Gill who were staying in
a posh hotel nearby so I had arranged to put my meagre
belongings, including dirty washing, in the café to lighten
my pack. As I got closer, I noticed the familiar, languid
figure of 'The Don' standing outside with an expresso
and the inevitable cigarette.

I was known as the Trappist monk at home (a man of few
words) but in line with my resolution to expand my comfort zone on this trip I decided to pluck up courage and
talk to him, after all I was fascinated. Within ten minutes
I had his life story, or the one he was prepared to share
with a stranger anyway. He was from the village but di-
vided his time between here and the South of France
(how accurate I had been in my guesswork the night before). He spoke fluent French which was handy as my

Spanish was still limited to asking for coffee, pizza and Aquarius which arrived with varying degrees of success. He was unimpressed with what I was trying to do and was more interested in talking about himself but wished me luck anyway and we said our goodbyes before I headed off into the café to get some rolls and coffee. 'The Don' re-appeared from his cigarette break and even agreed to keep an eye on my plastic bag. If only he knew what he was guarding.

I trotted off from the cafe and soon found the GR11 markings and a small path that led out of the village. The path was steep with patches of running water from a nearby stream - it was a bit like a very steep riverbed, complete with rocks, stones and water, if that makes sense. Before long my shoes were soaking wet and show-ing worrying signs of wear which only served to add to the dark cloud hanging over me. For space and weight reasons I had only been able to pack one pair and I knew that I was wildly optimistic thinking they would last 500 + miles in this terrain, particularly with the sharp granite shards of the Navarre mountains acting like razor blades.

But if I have one gift in life it is only to ever worry about the small things. My car could be driving over a cliff and

I would be fretting as to whether it was taxed or not. Both a curse and a blessing but perhaps more of the latter on this trip. So up and up I climbed, deep in thought.

The path was shrouded with a canopy of trees so there were no views to lighten my mood either. Never mind, I would use the time to work out the meaning of life, one of my favourite occupations. After an hour and a half I was no nearer to working out the meaning of life, but the path was levelling out and I burst through the canopy to be greeted with a beautiful plain complete with rainbow. The valley floor led up to the mountains and everywhere was a vivid green with hundreds of tiny waterfalls coming down from the snow capped peaks. Eureka! I could see the summit and I knew it was downhill all the way to my destination once I got to the top.

As I ran along the path to my right there was a huge commotion and at that moment two baby wild boars crashed out of the undergrowth and ran right across me squealing and crying. I whipped out my phone and tried to take a picture of this extraordinary sight before a thought crossed my mind ... experience suggested that, whatever the species, where there were two agitated babies there was probably an even more agitated mother not far behind. I really didn't fancy an encounter and decided to high tail it in the opposite direction as fast as my legs could carry me.

Once I had put a safe distance between me and the wildlife, not for the first time on the adventure, I took stock. I had lost the path - it was impossible to pick up with all the little rivulets coming down and had probably been washed away anyway. I was in such an isolated spot that perhaps no one had been here since last summer.

I looked up at the snow line and then down at my skimpy shorts and disintegrating shoes and then up at the snow line again. Something caught my eye - on the very top, through the low cloud, I could make out a steel tower. I recognised it, it was the top of a ski lift and where there was a ski lift there would be a piste nearby which would inexorably lead me down to the ski resort where no doubt I would be able to pick up the road.

Salvation! Without further ado I started the long trudge up the mountain picking my way as best I could through the little streams and trying to avoid the patches of snow I had given up all hope of salvaging my shoes but right now that was the least of my problems.

I finally got to the top and the foot of the ski lift pylon and my heart sank. It's difficult to describe but I'll do my best. The pylon was indeed the final pylon of the ski lift but it was perched on an outcrop of rock with the piste maybe 100 metres below. There was no way I could climb down without the use of ropes and to the left and right there was solid rock too, except … to my right I could see a patch of near vertical snow maybe 30 metres wide and to the right of that the ground looked a bit more accessible. If could just get across the ice wall then I'm sure I could climb, scramble, slide down to the piste and safety.

I gingerly made my way to the side of the wall and paused. One of the greatest attributes a person can have is fearlessness. Fearlessness in everything not just physical challenges but how we deal with people, circumstances and life itself. I had been trying to cultivate this for the last few years as I recognised the limitations that held me back from leading a rich, purposeful and fulfilling life. However I also knew that there is a difference between being fearless and being reckless.

I waited, my heart beating ever faster. Maybe I should re-trace my steps and try and traverse along the other side and then 'summit' further up. I waited ….

I faced the mountain on all fours, moved my foot to the left and 'cut' a step into the ice and snow as one would with a crampon although not with a disintegrating running shoe. But the snow wasn't too hard and I created a nice wide step and put my left foot into it and punched a small finger hold above. I moved the right foot into the step and repeated the whole process. I was now a metre from terra ferma and my fate was in the lap of the gods and my Hoka running shoes. I slowly made my way across. I could feel my whole body shaking with fear. About half way I paused and glanced down to my left. Fatal! Below I could see the rocks and if I fell now I would slide down and be dashed on them. Further down the mountain I could make out the specks of workmen in bright boiler suits working on the piste. I could even make out the starter's hut for the downhill course. Now was not the time for a geography lesson. Keep three limbs on the mountain at all times, three limbs, three limbs …. Finally, after what seemed an eternity although in reality was probably only ten minutes, the other side was in reach. One more step and I was on a grassy slope which I could slide and scramble down and join the piste.

I was elated and gave a whoop of joy. I ran down the piste and gave a bright and breezy "Hola" to the open mouthed workmen as I sped past. I stopped to take a picture of the starters hut of the downhill course before heading on downwards towards the deserted ski resort of Candenchu below. One for the memoirs - I would definitely want a memento of this day.

Ski resorts are funny places in summer - often grey, tired soulless buildings with grey, tired pavements waiting to be transformed by snow, bright lights and happy people. Candenchu was no exception and I swept though the enormous deserted car park onto the road that would take me across the dam towards Panticosa, the rendezvous point.

The view from the dam was spectacular and I could see the village maybe five kilometres below. I might even get to the rendezvous on time - my brother would be thrilled. I turned off the road onto a dirt track or camino that lead all the way into the village. I found a bar which sold the famous Aquarius and sat on an outside table in the sunshine drinking the tangy lemon drink and devouring ice cream waiting for Nick and Gill. Not quite *Ice*

Cold in Alex, the film made famous by John Mills, but my version of it.

I had somehow survived and you could even say thrived (there was definitely a renewed skip in my step) which is more than I could say for my shoes. The webbing had torn on both uppers and the soles were starting to disintegrate and offered no grip whatsoever. In fact they were darn right dangerous. The nearest big city was Pamplona, 100 miles away. What was I going to do? But do you know every day I was becoming more stoic in my outlook - what had happened to the worrier of old? There was nothing I could do about it at this precise moment so just enjoy the time to relax, something would turn up. And sure enough, at that moment, my brother and Gill arrived to take me to the hotel in Torla.

Torla was a picturesque village well geared for mountain tourism so there would be a chance that I would be able to find some new shoes although it would be unlikely they would be proper trail running shoes. I would just have to make do until I could find a bigger town. I had already explored the chances of getting Hoka to send me a pair, but moving ever eastwards with the minimum of planning it was impossible to find somewhere they could post them to. "Who on earth would be stupid enough to go on an expedition like this with only one pair of shoes?" I asked myself as I stared back at the weather beaten and gaunt face in the mirror.

Never mind, I felt better after a shower and a cleanish set of clothes. I even donned my waterproof trousers over my shorts to add a touch of mountaineer chic; after all no point in frightening the horses as they say.

Sure enough there was a mountain adventure store called La Tienda de Montana with an assortment of fabulous coats, ice axes and mountaineering packs in the window. I took a deep breath and entered. The assistant, who looked as though he spent his whole life on the mountain, looked me up and down taking in the raffish cut of the waterproofs, the torn running jacket and the disintegrating trail shoes. He smiled and I asked in perfect French if he spoke English. "Better than French" he said. "I am running across Spain in the footsteps of Kilian Jornet and my running shoes are kaput". He looked at me incredulously – "I'll get the manager". The manager was charming but didn't look too hopeful when I explained my predicament. "Hang on". He disappeared out the back and re-appeared a few minutes later clutching two boxes.

"These are the only two pairs in your size." I tried on the first pair which were more like walking boots. No good at all - it would take four men and a boy to help me lift my foot I thought. "No good". "Try these; they are very expensive but they were worn by (some unpronounceable namc) when he won the UTMB." And out of the box he took a beautiful pair of bright yellow and orange Dynastar running shoes. I slipped them on - "perfect".

They were eye wateringly expensive but he gave me 10% discount and threw in a pair of compression socks whatever they were.

I trotted off to the pizza place happy and content and I put the beautiful shoes on the table as I sipped a cold beer. "I'm probably going to sleep with these on" I thought to myself - "I love them".

As I sat on the bed later that evening, I thought of the amazing events that had befallen me on this, the most eventful of days. The fabulous valley, the squealing wild boar, the little waterfalls running down the mountain, the ski lift my saviour, the look on the workman's face as I ran down the piste, the view of the lake from the dam and of course my shoes. I also thought of the ice wall and made a mental note never to wish for a more eventful day again but to be happy with whatever presented itself and savour every moment however challenging.

Chapter 10

The Ordesa Valley

. . .

"Still round the corner, there may wait, a new road or a secret gate."

J.R.R Tolkien

I awoke early and the first sight that greeted me, lit by a shaft of light through the curtains, were my beautiful new shoes. I couldn't believe how lucky I had been to find them and with the vibrant yellow and orange colours I knew that people would certainly be able to find me.

I had done a lot of soul searching during the evening

about the adventure as a whole and I had come to several conclusions. Inwardly I knew that the target of completing the 500 mile trip in 21 days was not realistic. I couldn't believe how much climbing was involved. As I had mentioned before why was I so surprised? I would be climbing more than 120,000 feet over the 500 plus miles and for those of us imperially challenged that's the equivalent of four 'Everests'. And the highest peak (Aneto) was more than 11,000 feet. Kilian Jornet, who held the FKT (fastest known time) had done it in nine days but he was arguably the world's greatest mountain trail runner and I ... wasn't.

But I also knew from my eight marathons challenge that it was important to have some kind of target to aim at otherwise it was easy to 'drift' or to use ghastly 'corporate' speak; "lose focus and not achieve your goals". It sounds a paradox but I knew too, how easy it was make a mistake if you weren't absolutely pushing yourself to the limit and in these mountains that could be fatal.

I settled on a revised target of 28 days - it had a nice symmetry to it; an 'Everest' and 130 miles per week. A piece of cake.

To celebrate I put on a clean pair of socks taken from my washing line (aka a pair of shoe laces strung across the window frame) laced up the 'blister bunnies' as I had decided to christen my shoes and trotted happily down to breakfast.

I was to have a relatively quiet day today to give the shoes a chance to bed in and I would get to spend a bit of time with Nick and Gill who had been so supportive over the last couple of days. We were going to explore the Ordesa Valley, one of Spain's treasures and an area of outstanding beauty. I would still be heading eastwards and on the right track but it was only going to be about 14 miles with less than 2,000 feet of elevation and what's more I would probably get something to eat too.

The Ordesa Valley is part of the Ordesa y Monte Perdido National Park, a UNESCO World heritage site and part of the Ordesa-Viñamala UNESCO Biosphere . A bit of a mouthful but my goodness it certainly lived up to its billing and I think deserving of a short geography lesson too.

Right in the centre of the park is the limestone summit of Monte Perdido - the third highest peak in the Pyrenees at

3355m and a flavour of what was to come for me when I crossed into Andorra. There are, of course, several other summits of over 3,000 metres dotted along the Franco/Spanish border and I was going to experience every last one of them. The valley is formed of deep canyons and raised plateaux. The valley floor itself is green with pastures and woods and where the water forms waterfalls rush through canyons and gorges. In short it's stunning!

We set off together and climbed gently through the silver beech and fir woods with the majestic cliffs flanking us on either side. It wasn't long before, like a dog let off a lead, I was scurrying off in front and exploring in all directions, using the time to take some videos and pictures on my phone.

We passed several waterfalls, the sound of the rushing water deafening, before the woods opened up to lush meadows filled with flowers. There at the end of the valley far off in the distance was the Circo de Soasa waterfall with Monte Perdido dominating the skyline above. Of course I had to take a closer look and ran on ahead, arranging to meet Nick and Gill for a picnic at the end of the valley. Despite a small run-in with some cows blocking the path I made quick time to the waterfall and took a few pictures before taking myself off to the side of the valley where I sat on a rock in the sun. The holiday season hadn't started in earnest and there were only a few intrepid explorers who had made it this far but I still preferred to be on my own in this majestic place.

It wasn't long before the picnic arrived and whilst I can't remember exactly what it was I know that I probably had more than my fair share. After all food at lunchtime - this was both a novelty and a treat.

We started the long trek back to the car park and I decided to run on ahead to test the shoes and write up some notes. Nick was going to veer off a steep path which afforded magnificent views of the whole valley and Gill was to press on and complete her half marathon.

You're probably wondering how I was getting on with the shoes. Well in one word - fantastic! They were heavier than the Hokas but so comfortable and not a trace of any hot spots or blisters - maybe I would have to call them something else, for 'Blister Bunnies' they were not. It wasn't recommended practice to run 15 miles in a brand new pair of shoes but I had got away with it and besides I didn't have much choice.

I got back to the car park and to my delight saw that there was a shop open that sold ice creams - what a treat. I bought the biggest that I could find and retired to the river bank to sit on a stone and ponder life. As I sat there in the sunshine, my senses filled with the sound of the water burbling and babbling in the background I reflected on the difference of being alone and being lonely. It was very easy to be surrounded by people and feel lonely and conversely to be alone and feel absolutely at peace and not lonely at all. And I think this was my state in these beautiful life-changing mountains.

Enough philosophising there were ice creams to be had for half marathoners and intrepid explorers and who knows I might even be able to persuade them that, just for a change, pizza should be on the menu tonight.

Chapter 11

Orla the dog …

"Your body is not a temple, it's an amusement park. Enjoy the ride."

Anthony Bourdain

S uitably refreshed after a good night sleep I slipped out of the hotel and sought out the ever-familiar GR11 chevrons that would lead me to Farno. I had loaded Spain in Google maps last night and couldn't believe that Andorra was in my sights. I looked on Andorra as my halfway point although, me being me, I hadn't bothered to actually calculate if that was fact. I had managed to smuggle a piece of pizza from the restaurant the night before and chewed on this thoughtfully as I studied the large map which could normally be found at the start of the trail.

As usual I was completely alone except for two bus drivers smoking their morning cigarette as they waited patiently for 'Ordesa customers'. I did my "Buenos" and trotted off happily down a well made-up track towards Broto where I would join the trail proper.

After an hour I got to the village of Broto without incident and headed along the river looking for the GR11 sign that would take me East. I arrived at a large map in a small square by the river, got my bearings and set off on the long climb to the next summit. I had noticed an Alsatian in the square – I had learnt to have a healthy respect for all dogs on this trip but particularly Alsatians and runners represented a nice moving target for them to aim for. Although I was tired my legs felt strong and I was moving at a good clip along the gently rising path before the climb proper where I knew my pace would slow to a crawl.

I had been climbing for about half an hour up the narrow path with a spectacular drop to my left when I sensed that I was not alone; I often had these feeling on the mountains even though I sometimes didn't see a soul all day. But this time it was different, more powerful. I looked behind me – nothing. I kept going but the feeling of not being alone wouldn't leave me. I turned round again and looked down the narrow path to see the Alsatian from the village less than 50 mctrcs behind me. What an earth was he doing here? I was sure that he had been with a couple when I was in the square. Every time I turned round he stopped but each time, like a game of cat and mouse, he was ever closer until eventually he was right behind me. I stopped and tried to shoo him down the mountain but he wouldn't budge and stuck a couple of paces behind me each time stopping as I stopped. What should I do? Should I take him back to his owners? But I was already more than an hour from the village. Would he go back on his own accord. As I pondered this a couple of hikers came down the mountain towards me. This was unusual in itself but it would be a godsend; they could take the dog down to Broto to be reunited with its owners and I could keep going on what was going to be a long, hard day.

After exchanging pleasantries I told them my story about the dog. "Oh don't worry" said the man, "There are tales of dogs in these mountains following travellers for days –

he will return home when he feels like it". Great! My
mind raced – what was I going to do with him tonight
when and if I found somewhere to stay. Would we end up
huddled in a shelter somewhere. As I bought myself back
to the present moment I realised that the couple had departed and the dog was sitting at my feet.

I rummaged in my rucksack and took out a battered flapjack which we shared and then I poured some of my precious water into the cup of my hand which he licked happily. "Well if we are going to be travelling companions
you're going to need a name … how about Orla, I like
that". And so it was that Orla and his new friend started
climbing again.

After another 45 minutes we ran through a deserted hill
top hamlet before coming to a point where two paths
crossed. I sat down and we shared the last of the flapjack
and had another sip of water. I knew we had to press on
but Orla had other ideas. He was lying across the narrow
path and wouldn't let me go forward – if I sat down he
sat down, if I got up to go he lay across my feet and
wouldn't budge. It was like he was trying to tell me
something but what? I was sitting on a little hummock,

my back resting against a post on the path crossroads. I turned and noticed there was a battered sign at the top of the post with a name carved in wood. I'm sure the name rang a bell … and then it dawned on me the name of the village was to the West – I was going 180 degrees the wrong way.

I turned tail and as one Orla got up and was again padding in my footsteps a respectful yard or two behind me although it was he who should be leading the way as he had a far better sense of direction than me. As I descended I tried to make sense of what had just taken place – had the dog really followed me to put me back on track in all senses of the word? After all, I knew from previous experience and in particular the eight marathons expedition that the early stages of an adventure was the danger period for wanting to quit. I'll never know but I like to think that he was sent to me that day and as the trip got to the latter stages I often thought back to Orla, that very special dog.

You probably want to know what became of Orla? Well we got down close to the square and there was his owner sitting patiently on a wall waiting for him. I was glad to re-unite them and I swear as I left them, Orla turned and gave me one last glance as if to say "go on you can do it".

I stopped at a grubby little bar at the crossroads which I had left a couple of hours ago for some water and then set off in the right direction … probably. I've already described how depressing it can be for an ultra-runner to have to retrace his steps but in this case my mood was upbeat for the experience of meeting Orla. In fact, not even the disgruntled, unfriendly barman could upset my equilibrium.

It wasn't long before once again I was climbing, this time eastwards and in the right direction. Although I had time to make up I felt elated after the 'Orla' experience, I had got plenty of water and on paper at least the route looked fairly straightforward. As I got to the top and stopped to catch my breath, I looked behind me from where I had come and in the far distance I could see the other peak that I had already climbed. I started the descent passing through a deserted village as I reached the valley floor. This wasn't the first deserted village I had come across but there was something sinister about this one. The buildings were in better repair than some of the other ones I had passed through. It was as if the inhabitants had just stopped what they were doing and left en masse. The shell of the chapel was on a slope sulking in the shadows. I didn't hang around and was glad to be on the path out of the village and heading towards the rendezvous.

It's hard to explain the anxiety that a lack of sense of direction brings. I knew that one wrong turn here would mean a night on the mountains and worse still probably in the deserted village. Probably a bit of an afterthought now but I resolved to learn how to read a map and use a compass properly ... but then again, half the fun of an adventure is the step into the unknown.

The shadows were lengthening as I crossed the stream and started what I hoped would be the last climb. By now I was really tired and was struggling just to keep moving. My mood wasn't lifted when I saw the skull of a cow nailed to the tree - there really was something dark about this area and I had read about tales of witchcraft dating back centuries. The never-ending climb got steeper and steeper and the unused path was overgrown with the brush and foliage clinging onto me like an octupses' tentacles.

Now when you feel like this there are two approaches you can take; the first and well tried approach is to sit on the side of the path blubbing your eyes out and feeling sorry for yourself. And dear reader you will know this is normally my preferred option. However on this occasion I decided to employ my 'marathon' approach. This involves quickening your pace and shouting expletives to yourself (If any readers were spectators at the Brighton marathon let me apologise retrospectively for my disgraceful language in the closing stages). Anyway it seemed to do the trick and as I crashed through the undergrowth with a string of expletives and before long I could hear my brother calling anxiously from the top.

We found a magical little bar with fabulous views over the Pyrenees and I told Nick and Gill about my exploits (missing out my temper tantrum) over an ice cold beer.

It was to be our last night together so we celebrated with, yes you've guessed it - pizza as we looked at the route options for the next day. I've already highlighted my brother's prowess with maps and I was going to need his skills to plan the next part of the adventure. The snow was still lying quite deep on the next section and with my lack of any kind of cold weather gear it would be madness to try the Haut Pyrenees route so I would head down and along the valley for 30 miles or so and then head back up the mountain. It would add a little bit of mileage to the trip but what was 30 miles in the scope of things when you were going to do more than 500.

As I lay in bed gathering my thoughts in the moonlight, I saw the pack on the back of the chair winking at me. Oh yes I had forgotten about that - deep joy we were going to be reunited - every last kilo of her in the morning. My eyes closed and I was gone into a world of deserted chapels, cows' skulls and handsome Alsatians.

Chapter 12

Alone again …

"When everything is lonely I can be my best friend."

Conor Oberst

Nick and Gill took me to Fanlo, my stopping off point from the previous evening, and as we said our goodbyes I realised I was, in the immortal words of Gilbert O'Sullivan, "alone again naturally". Of course I had another reminder in the form of my 7.5 kg rucksack on my back.

It's hard to explain, I had been so grateful of all their help and support, but there was a part of me that wanted to be alone again in these magnificent mountains and continue to find out a bit more about myself. It's a paradox but so few of us actually get to spend time alone to get to know ourselves and that's a pretty essential part of living a happy and free life.

Today was going to be a relatively easy day without too much climbing and part of the route to Escalona would take me on a spectacular single track, mountain road. Well that's how Nick had patiently described it on the map. Where I would actually end up would be anyone's guess. The way marking down to the village of Nerin was tricky but I didn't get lost and it wasn't long before I waved goodbye to the GR11 and the blue, red and white chevrons for a couple of days. I really was in uncharted territory now.

I knew at some point there would be a turning off the path which would take me down an escarpment into a hidden valley before climbing again and up onto the mountain road. I could hear the rush of water but no turn off. Now I don't know if any of you have seen the film *McKenna's Gold* starring Gregory Peck (if not this point will be a bit lost on you but I'll press on anyway). In the film there is a hidden valley full of gold which can only be discovered through a narrow passage way highlighted when the sun shines on it. Well this was my *McKenna's*

Gold moment - beside an enormous rock there was a narrow gap, barely wide enough to fit through, and there, behind the rock, was a path which quite literally was on the edge of a precipice. This snaked down several hundred feet into the valley and the waterfall below. No health and safety here, just an enormous drop into the valley below. I've got a good head for heights but even I was slightly perturbed at the steepness and narrowness of the path and I took great care in navigating it.

Now to understand the next part of my story I need to take you back a bit - in fact 55 years to the plains of the Serengeti and my childhood in Africa. I was too small to be left at home so my mother and I used to accompany my father on the innumerable safaris he took. Nowadays most people's vision of a safari is white, shiny, 4 x 4s travelling in convoy with lots of excited tourists snapping the wildlife from the safety of the trucks before heading back to luxury accommodation for their gin and tonics and steaks. In the sixties our version of a safari was very different. Our convoy consisted of my father's Landrover and an old battered truck which would carry the supplies, medicines etc. as well as the helpers and Ascari (scouts) who would work with my father on the trip. The trips could easily last a week or more and we would set up camp each evening in the bush or we would sleep under the stars in a Masai boma. It's hard to believe, I know, but I was a very active, adventurous and inquisitive child and for this reason the driver of the truck Imbaraku, was designated to keep a 24-hour watch on me. Imbaraku was a 'mzei', swahili for wise old man and was probably the most sensible out of all of us which is how he landed the plum job of looking after me. If he couldn't keep me out of harm's way then no one could. We were inseparable. But wise as Imbaraku was I do remember vividly Mum gently telling the two of us off for catching snakes with a fork stick near the camp.

So back to the Pyrenees and with my upbringing in mind you will be surprised at my reaction to the snake that I came across on that narrow, steep path. I let out a shriek and vaulted over it before careering down the path at full speed with rocks and stones scattering into the ravine below. It was a full 25 metres before I stopped to gather myself and slow my pounding heart. By the time I got to the bottom all thoughts of the snake were banished as I marvelled at the stunning water cascades and the deep emerald pools. As I mentioned earlier, I had a relatively short day planned of about 17 miles with 2,500 feet of climb and with this in mind, I took the opportunity to lie on a flat rock. I shut my eyes and felt the sun warm my aching bones as I let the sound of the cascading water wash over me - paradise.

I don't know how long I lay there, probably only a few minutes, but I felt relaxed and galvanised at the same time. I heaved on the running vest (it sounds lighter than rucksack) and trotted along the river before I started the climb out of the other side of the gorge. The ascent was neither as steep nor as precarious as the descent and mercifully 'snakeless' too. Before long I emerged onto the single track road which skirted the escarpment and would eventually take me to the village of Escalona. It made a real difference to run on an even surface and gently downhill at that so I made good time and enjoyed the novel experience of not arriving at dusk or worse.

So it was with a jaunty step that I approached the reception desk of the rather tired hotel and gave the man on reception my best beaming 'break the ice' smile. The man scowled at me as he looked me up and down with disdain. I sensed we were not going to be friends and how right I was. He looked tired, hungover and extremely cross at having been disturbed from his afternoon nap. I marked him down immediately as a classic 'Sales Prevention Agent' from the genus "I don't give a flying f**k" more commonly found in establishments and help centres up and down the country back at home. We went through the charade of him pretending not to understand me and losing my booking, which I had made the night before with Nick, before he begrudgingly checked my email confirmation and miraculously found my booking, Then he announced, in perfect English, with great glee that the restaurant would not be available as they had a large function and I would not be able to get anything to eat. Now it's very important in life to never let a bully get the last word. "That's great because I'm on a 48 hour fast anyway" I proudly announced before turning sharply on my heel and heading for the stairs and then turning sharply back again to return to the desk and pick up my key.

After my shower I couldn't wait to get out of the hotel and try and find something to eat. In the event I found a nice cafe with WIFI where not only did I get a chance to catch up on my notes and emails but also devour a delicious goats cheese salad and a pudding of indeterminate origin. There were other adventurers too a very friendly Irishman and his friend who were doing the GR11 traverse and we swopped tales of the trails over a cold beer.

I returned to the hotel and the refuge of my room before sinking into my bed and listening to the sounds of the drunken revellers below.

Chapter 13

Running on the edge

. . .

"If you think adventure is dangerous, try routine; it is lethal."
Paulo Coelho

I t was still dark outside as I put on my running gear for the umpteenth time. It was only day 11 of my journey across the Pyrenees but I felt as if I had been running for ever. Although it was early, I was glad to be leaving the hotel. It was one of the very few places that I had stayed where the staff had not been friendly and besides, I had a lot of climbing to do today as I was leaving the valley and heading back up the mountain.

No breakfast but I was getting used to that. But as I traversed up the side of the river, the early morning mist lifted and the sun came out which made me feel a whole lot better. I decided that I even had time to bask on a rock for 15 minutes and let the sun warm my tired bones. I searched the pockets of the rucksack in the vain hope that there was a scrap of food there – perhaps a bit of congealed chocolate or a half eaten flapjack. No, the cupboard was bare. Breakfast would have to wait.

For once all the path markings seemed to be clear and it was with relative ease that I reached Lafortunada which appeared to be completely deserted. By this time I would have eaten absolutely anything so it was with some relief that I found a builder working on a house who pointed me in the direction of the one and only café. I rustled up two cups of strong coffee which came with a miniature muffin and seeing the haggard look on my face the owner gave me an extra couple for luck. It was so comfortable here but I remembered the ultra runners mantra "beware of the chair" and reluctantly heaved my rucksack onto my back and waved goodbye to the owner. I saw the nice builder on the way back to the path and with some hesitation offered him one of my precious muffins … unfortunately he gratefully accepted it. Never mind, perhaps my generosity would be rewarded later in the day.

The sun was beating down now, but suitably refreshed and with full water bottles and a stomach that had stopped grumbling I pressed on. Up and up I climbed with the path getting ever more precarious; in some places it was perhaps no more than a metre wide and so exposed that it was hacked into the side of the mountain and the edge reinforced with tree trunks. One false step here and that would be it. It was strange but I can honestly say, with one or two exceptions, that I very rarely thought of the danger which was probably just as well.

So what did I think about when I was on these stages? For the most part, particularly at the start of the day, my mind was a mass of calculations. I knew that the last thing I could afford was to be stranded on the mountain after nightfall so all the variables where fed in – how fast was I going, what was the climb like, where was a likely stopping point, how much water was I using, where would the next water point or stream be etc. By early afternoon my thought pattern would have changed depending on where I was. So, from "oh f**k it I'm not going to make it, I'll have to sleep under a boulder", to "God I'm hungry" or more often than not "this is the most beautiful place I've ever been".

Finally, I reached the top and started the steep descent into Sarvillo where I was sure I would find something to eat and a chance to get my bearings. Well, I was right on one count – No food but there was a sign which reliably informed me that the route to Plan and my proposed night stop would take eight hours walking. So even if I could knock an hour or two off that on the bits I could run I calculated I would be there about 10:30pm – not good news. So once again it was decision time. There was a road, that I calculated, would get me there before nightfall if I could go at a reasonable pace.

The decision was made and it was with a purposeful stride that I ran past the sign on the side of the road that read "NO CAMINE POR LA PISTA". The road was fairly wide with a little verge that I could hop onto on the rare occasions that a car or lorry approached me. As the road climbed up the side of the mountain, the drop to my left got steeper and steeper and there was now a solid

112

rock wall on the right side of the road too. But I wasn't unduly concerned as I was facing the on-coming traffic and the traffic was light. That all changed when, to my horror, I saw a sign announcing that a tunnel was ahead. I stopped at the entrance and considered my options – on my left was deep ravine and to my right a shear rock face so it was either turn back and try and find a barn or shed to sleep in, or go through the tunnel. No choice really. I tilted my head to hear if there was any traffic approaching and then took off up the road at a rate of knots and into the dark tunnel. It was an eerie feeling, but the tunnel was short and in no time I emerged into the bright sunlight and the relative safety of the open road. What was I worrying about? I was not lost for once, I was going to make my destination before it got dark and I was definitely going to get something to eat.

I passed through another short tunnel without incident before coming to a bend in the road and yet another tunnel. What made this one different was that I couldn't see the light at the other end so it was likely to be much longer than the others. I was near the top of the mountain now, so the drop to my left was probably more than 1,000 feet and of course there was the shear wall of the mountain on the other side. I noticed too that the traffic was getting heavier with one or two lorries added to the mix – perhaps it was approaching the end of the working day.

There was no turning back now, so I gathered myself for one final sprint. I was wearing black shorts, a dark T-shirt and my pack was black so I put on my jacket which had some faded fluorescent patches which just might be picked up by any oncoming lights. A final deep breath and I was off. I ran as fast as my tired legs could carry me into the darkness of the tunnel. But then my worst fears were realised – I heard behind me the deep exhaust of, what sounded like, a large truck as simultaneously I saw the faint glow of lights off the walls of the tunnel as a car approached. If they didn't see me this would be it. There was no way that there would be room for a lorry, a car and a human too and besides, what idiot would be running through a tunnel dressed in black with no light.

I would like to say that my life flashed before me, that I thought of all the things that I hadn't said or done, all the people I was going to leave behind. But in fact my only thought was "bugger – not even half way". I ripped my pack off and pressed myself as flat as I could into the cold walls of the tunnel just as the lorry and the car approached. I swear I felt the caress of the wing mirror as the lorry and car crossed paths and disappeared into the distance. I grabbed my pack and ran like hell for the light at the end of the tunnel and it was at least two minutes before I emerged. I unceremoniously ran to the side of the road and threw up.

I sat on the Armco, chest heaving, composing myself before continuing. After a few metres I turned onto a track which would take me across the dam and into Plan where a hot bath, a hot meal and a warm bed awaited me.

As I entered Plan I spotted the welcoming beacon of a café. I hadn't eaten anything since the muffins in the morning, and those had been deposited on the side of the road anyway, so I was absolutely famished. The café was warm and welcoming, so different from the hotel the day before, with a lovely owner who was keen to practice her English and made me feel really welcome. No disdain at my dishevelled appearance but just encouragement and awe when she heard my story and what I was trying to do. She didn't bat an eyelid either when I ordered two delicious looking doughnuts sitting on the counter, a brace of Aquarius, a strong coffee and a tall beer. It's amazing what the warmth of a complete stranger can bestow - a real lesson for me and one that I was determined to cultivate and practice.

We chatted like old friends for half an hour or so before I realised it was dark and I needed to check into the hotel. I was invited back later as Spain were playing in the football world cup and the bar would be buzzing and "yes" they did serve pizza.

I followed the Señora's directions and within minutes I was waiting at the reception desk of the most swanky, luxurious hotel you can imagine. I don't want to cast aspersions on Plan, this most friendly of villages, but I was surprised what my 40 euros got me to say the least. The room was enormous with a huge king size bed and the bathroom - well. This was to be a first. Rather than a traditional hotel bathroom this actually had a jacuzzi. After a few false starts, with sprays and jets of water spraying all and sundry, I settled down into what was certainly the most luxurious bath I'd ever had. After an age, and with wrinkled and scrubbed skin, I reluctantly pulled myself out and did a bit of 'Masai washing' before hanging up my clothes on my 'patented' shoe lace washing line to dry.

I wanted to create a good impression for my new friends so I carefully selected a cleanish T-shirt, my best shorts (without the rip in the crotch) and even wiped off the dried mud from my over trousers. I inspected myself in the mirror. Never mind it would have to do.

As I entered the bar; the noise was deafening and the place was rammed with excited football fans. I was amazed how everyone was involved from old to young, so different from the culture back home. There were no tables but the patron found me a stool at the bar and I tucked into an enormous pizza and a custard pudding washed down with ice cold beer.

During the evening various customers came up to me and shook my hand which touched me deeply. It's hard to explain, but as I've alluded to before, I'm rarely lonely when I'm alone but often lonely when I'm in a crowded place. That was not the case here and I shall never forget the welcome and kindness I was shown although I'm ashamed that I forgot the owner's name. When this book is published, I shall return and hand over a signed copy which she can give to unruly customers to read as a penance.

Chapter 14

Spectacles, testicles, wallet and watch …

"He would travel happily must travel light."
Antoine De St. Exupery

Perhaps refreshed is the wrong word but I definitely woke feeling rested. I decided to spoil myself and have breakfast in the hotel but not before I indulged in another jacuzzi.

As I sat down to coffee, rolls and jam I caught up with emails and a bit of social media. I was shocked to see that 'Marathon Man', who was attempting a world record run across America, had been accused of cheating and taking rides in his support vehicle. How sad - I wondered if, in the unlikely event I completed this adventure, I would be accused of cheating. After all a directionally challenged, 60-year-old man, dressed in tattered running shorts and carrying his belongings in a little rucksack, running 500 miles across the Pyrenees did sound a bit far-fetched. I suppose any suspicious journalist could always spend a day with me on the mountains I mused ... mind you I hope they have a head for heights.

I asked the lovely hotelier if I could have a forage in her kitchen and she packed me off with some fruit and a couple of plain rolls. With my water bottles full, I somewhat reluctantly set off for another day of thrills, spills and adventure although I hoped that perhaps it wouldn't be quite so eventful as the previous one.

As I wended my way from the village, up a wide logging track, I noticed a distinct change in the weather. It was a lot colder and the skies, a leaden grey, looked heavy with rain or worse. For once I decided to be proactive and found a tree stump on the side of the track to empty the rucksack. I then decided to wear most of the contents including gloves, over trousers and waterproof top. Then followed the ritual of the 'double check' - 'spectacles, testicles, wallet and watch'. Although in my case I was more interested in the passport. A few days earlier, when I had been searching for any vestiges of food, the passport had fallen out onto the dry track and it was sheer chance that I had spotted it. Thank God for the bright red of the passport cover - at least I'd got something out of the EU.

Suitably attired, and with a considerably lighter rucksack, I set off ever upwards at precisely the same moment as it started to sleet. Great! There was no getting away from it; I was feeling decidedly down. It wasn't just the weather either. I had been running, walking, scrambling for 11 days and I had covered a distance of 227 miles and climbed 42,966 feet. I was constantly hungry and often dehydrated and this was the easy part - I still had the challenge of Andorra to come. As I trudged up the steep track, I gave myself the standard pep talk, about how lucky I was to be able to do this, how beautiful the place was, I wasn't injured, etc. But nothing worked. So I retreated into the ultra runners refrain "one foot in front of the other, one foot in front of the other". I was very interested in the whole concept of willpower - most ultra runners are and I knew that there was a lot more to it than "you can do it".

Finally after three and a half hours I emerged from the thickly wooded track onto a broad ridge and the summit. It was incredibly windy but at least the rain was replaced with sunshine. To my amazement I spotted two hikers on the ridge lying down to rest (I think) in a little hollow in the lea of the mountain. They were as surprised to see me as I was them but showing true British reserve, I gave a quick smile and moved swiftly on my way.

As I started the long descent, I found a sheltered rock to sit on and have my impromptu picnic garnered from the hotel's kitchen that morning. Although I was feeling much happier with my lot I thought I would try some meditation in this most beautiful of spots. I had read so much about the benefits, watched endless YouTube videos and had tried to practice it too but had never got the hang of it. If I couldn't do it here in these surroundings, with no one about except me and the cows, then there was no hope. I got comfortable and closed my eyes and listened to the gentle tinkering of the cow bells. "This is quite relaxing - I wonder how long it's going to take me to do the next section - will I be able to cross into Andorra if there's too much snow - I wonder if they will have anything that's not meat in the hotel tonight - will I even find the hotel tonight - why haven't I got any blisters yet? I should do, perhaps I'm not going to - I'm sure those bells are getting closer". My eyes snapped open - It's no good I was never going to be able to do this.

I re-packed my rucksack checking that there were no morsels of food left and that I had cleared up my rubbish. 'Spectacles, testicles, wallet and watch … and passport' and I was off.

I flew down the mountain on the narrow path and it was blissful. Not a care in the world, just the wind in my face the sun on my back and all I had to do was place my feet - pitter patter, pitter patter. And then I understood … in the words of Jon Kabat Zim "Meditation, it's not what you think".

Down and down I went until I reached the tiny village of Chia whose only inhabitants seemed to be a herd of maybe ten cows grazing in a little paddock behind an old stone wall. As one they approached the wall and just stared at me. Now you'll remember I'm distinctly nervous of cows but these were different - maybe it was knowing they were behind the wall, but they seemed friendly and curious rather than aggressive and threatening. I stored this information in the memory bank; maybe this was their natural state and in any case it had put a smile on my face. My smile got even broader when I found a tiny bar with a handsome dog on guard and more importantly cans of cold Aquarius - my secret Pyrenean weapon.

Thirst slaked, water bottles full, dog patted, hotel sorted and I was off on the final descent to Casteljon and the lavishly named Hotel Rural Plaza.

That evening as I sat down with a cold beer I went through my notes and worked out the progress I had made and reflected how far I had come metaphorically and physically. There had definitely been some progress. I used to be able to worry for Britain - every conceivable nightmare scenario would be played out in my head. If I was going to a meeting sometimes I would arrive over an hour early to bypass the non-existent train derailment, police incident or road closures. If I saw a child or old person walking I would be ready at a moment's notice to catch them when they tripped on the pavement (which I was more likely to do than them). I had to sit with my back to a wall and in the same place in the coffee shop every day and if my routine was disturbed that would set me back for the whole day. I would do anything, often to my detriment to please people and make them like me. And then there was the now …. half the time no idea where I was let alone where I was going. Hotels and hostels booked-half an hour before I rocked up if at all. Completely ill-prepared in terms of clothing and equipment (although I had grown to love my shoes, shorts and yes even the rucksack). Running solo for hours with little or no food in the wilderness on precarious mountain tracks drinking out of streams shared with the cows and heavens knows what else.

And do you know what? … I loved it, every last minute of it, even when I was blubbing on the side of the track feeling sorry for myself. Yes, this was living.

Chapter 15

Motorway running

. . .

"It feels good to be lost in the right direction."

Anon

I am not quite sure at what stage of the day I realised the route I had planned was on the motorway but it was certainly within the first half hour. I had 'previous' of course. I had run a marathon in Lisbon, taken a wrong turn and ended up on the E1. I knew something wasn't right when I was running on the hard shoulder with cars hooting and flashing their lights and I was forced to leg it over a fence through a private wood to avoid the police. This wasn't my only experience of 'motorway running' I decided to run across Italy in 2017 and again took a wrong turning but this time I actually got my name in lights "danger man in road" in two languages before I realised my mistake. (I still have the picture to prove it). What was particularly impressive about the Italian episode was that it was only two kilometres from the start and I still had another 298 km to go.

I digress but suffice it to say that I decided to have a rethink on the route. I saw my mistake and managed to circumnavigate back onto the GR18. It was badly marked and hardly used but so beautiful with lush pastures giving way to a tricky wooded section before the inevitable endless climb.

But somehow it was different from yesterday - I felt strong after a good night sleep, although I'd had little food and I was definitely feeling more chipper. Perhaps it was my improved navigation skills that had avoided 'motorwaygate' or just the vibrant colours in the sunshine. Whatever it was I was grateful. I hopped over streams countless times and I had my first proper encounter with the mosquitos that, together with the flies, were to become a feature as the trip wore on. As I climbed ever further upwards on the narrow path I came to yet another deserted village. Then, as I rounded a bend, I was greeted by an extraordinary sight. There, right in front of me, was an enormous, elderly horse completely on his own, straddled across the path. I don't think I'd ever seen such an elderly horse and me being me, as with Orla the dog, I looked for a sign. Was the horse a good omen to show me that I was on the right track or maybe with his size a spiritual guide to guard over me. After careful consideration the only conclusion that I came to was he looked as old and knackered as I felt. We said our goodbyes and I continued on my merry way.

Finally the path burst onto a little road which in turn, and rather incongruously, led to a tired and rather grubby café. Needless to say I was the only customer but I think I made up for the days takings with my order off three bottles of lemonade and two snickers bars which I wolfed down in double quick time. The owner assured me that the path to Castaneda was just ahead, off the road, and I was on the right route. To my dismay I realised it was a lot further than I thought. There was nothing for it - I would have to go hell for leather to make it by nightfall. So with a cheery "Gracias" I was out of the door and on my way again.

There's a wonderful saying, attributed to John Muir , that goes something like this; "off to the forest I go to lose my mind and find my soul". I often thought about this, substituting 'mountains' for 'forest'. It absolutely encapsulates the spirit of the adventure and it was how I had felt all morning. But there were other times, like when getting lost or traversing the ice wall, that a switch flicks on and your senses go from green to amber to red in a blink of an eye. Now was such a moment. I knew that the timings were going to be tight to get to the one and only hotel I had found on my Google search the previous night.

Sure enough, exactly as the barman had promised, I found the track and I was off, scampering over the terrain and making good time. I flashed past a sign indicating 'beware of the cows' (or was it a bull - probably need to work that out before the end of the trip) although the tinkling of the cow bells told me all I needed to know. I came to a tiny hamlet, maybe just two or three houses with no sign of life and where the GR18 just seemed to peter out in someone's garden. I got my phone out – Yes! I had a signal. I was definitely on the right track and my destination was round the rim of the valley, maybe only two or three miles away. As I approached the garden gate two snarling dogs leapt up. This couldn't be right. I must have taken a wrong turn somewhere. Another dilemma - I was exhausted. I had already climbed in excess of 5,000 feet and run over 20 miles and my destination was almost within touching distance. But there was the lack of the path, not to mention the dogs too. Never mind where there is a problem there is a solution …. usually.

I remembered I had a signal so I should be able to plot my path right across the valley and not bother to go around the rim. Although there would be a bit of climbing the other side of the valley it would probably be shorter, I told myself. So the Ernest Shackleton of the Pyrenees set off at full tilt clutching his trusty phone. It was probably within two minutes that the phone signal went and the map disappeared, maybe sooner. But never mind I had taken some bearings and I was sure I could see where I was trying to get to.

An hour later I was still on the valley floor, completely lost with my route barred on all sides. I was absolutely furious with myself - why hadn't I had the guts to face the dogs or at least try and find someone in the houses who could put me back on the right track? I caught myself - self admonishment wasn't the answer - there were enough people who could do that for me without me doing it to myself. No! Time to get my game face on and find a way out of here. The switch I mentioned earlier had well and truly switched to red and despite the tiredness my mind was fully engaged. There would be a road into the valley so if I went along the valley floor I was sure to find it and then I could take the road out on the other side. It would be longer but a lot safer in the dark than thrashing through the undergrowth in circles.

And so it proved to be. Another hour later and I was on top of the valley, on the correct side this time and on a single track road with a sign to the village. Sure enough, a few kilometres later and three hours after the debacle with the dogs I arrived at the entrance to the hotel just as the last rays of the sun disappeared behind the mountains.

I walked into an enormous bar area which doubled as the hotel's reception to be greeted by the Patron and a local who looked very familiar to me. "We didn't think you were going to come - did you have trouble finding us?" "You could say that" I replied although I think the subtlety was lost in translation. I ordered two Aquarius lemonades and a beer which seemed to impress the local. Then it came to me why he was so familiar - about two kilometres back, when I had joined the road, he had nearly run me over in his pickup. "You're the only guest but I'll fetch the girl and she will make you some food and I'll show you to your room". "She speaks English too". Sure enough, while the barman chatted to his friend, a friendly looking girl appeared from the back. Maybe it was his daughter, there was certainly a resemblance and in the matter of fact speaking too. "You are the only guest but I will make you some supper, what would you like?". "Well I'm vegetarian (I had long ago given up all hopes of maintaining a vegan diet on this trip) so anything along those lines" I replied. She thought long and hard; "Tuna salad". "Perfect - thank you".

"Come on, I'll show you to your room" and with that the Patron took me through a labyrinth of corridors to a nice room with large shutters and a huge bed. "Do you like cows?" He asked. "Well actually I'm a bit frightened of them". "That's a pity" he said with a mischievous smile "because one of the largest herds in Europe is going to go right past your window at six tomorrow morning."

After a shower and a bit of 'Masai washing' I picked out my outfit for the night. The overtrousers were caked in mud so my bright blue shorts with a hole in the crutch it

132

would be. I returned to the bar and chatted with the bar-man while I picked at my salad. I think when he realised what I was trying to do he felt as bit guilty about allocat-ing me the 'cow room' but I didn't mind - I was going to be up early and we departed friends; and me with the contents of the fruit bowl in my rucksack.

Chapter 16

Ants in your pants

. . .

"If ants are so busy how come they find time to go to all the picnics."

T.S Elliot

True to his word at 6:00 am on the dot there was a cacophony of noise getting ever closer as hundreds and hundreds of cows made their way along the bleached track a few feet from my ground floor window. Each with a bell around its neck. But I already had a march on them and was up and ready to go. It was at least 15 minutes before the bells faded off into the distance and I was able to escape my lair. Luckily I was heading in the opposite direction but I still had the cow pats to dodge in the morning light and of course with the cows came the flies - millions of them. Every time I approached a cow pat I disturbed them and I found myself running through a black mist before the next cow pat. Several thousand of them thought I was a better bet than the cows and they followed me buzzing around my face, ears, eyes, mouth - in fact everywhere you can think of.

Luckily I'd always had a pretty good immune system (maybe something about my Africa days - after all Mum was pretty liberally minded when it came to feeding us) so despite swallowing the odd one I fancied my chances.

The path wound around the side of the valley and as I looked down, I could see a tiny croft nestling in the valley below. Just imagine living there surrounded by this day after day ... minus the flies of course - heaven.

With one final wistful glance, me and the the flies found the path and the inevitable climb up to the ridge far in the distance. The path seemed to merge with a rocky creek surrounded by a canopy of trees and I kept going. As long as I was continuing to climb I must be going in the right direction I surmised. But the markings disappeared and I realised I was lost. No heroics; I descended the creek and found the markings again. I was totally disorientated and for a moment just couldn't work out in what direction I should be going. I felt completely isolated and out of sorts - was I coming down with something?

I had forgotten to put my hat on and was getting really burnt, perhaps this was the cause of my distress? I was bushwhacking up the path - so much effort for so little reward. The markings were very poor (I guess no one ever came up here) and as I came to a derelict shepherd's hut, not for the first time, I realised I had wandered off the path, such as it was, and was hopelessly lost. I could see where I was trying to get to but there was probably 50 metres of dense shrub and stinging nettles between me and what I hoped would be the path.

No big deal you might think but I should point out that amongst my many phobias, I have a thing about stinging nettles. As a seven-year-old I was thrown into a huge patch of nettles by the school bullies and I have never looked on them the same since. But I had spent too much of my life looking backwards and I was determined that this trip was about moving forwards. I launched myself into the undergrowth and head down crashed through the detritus towards the sanctuary of the clearing and what I hoped would be the markers for the GR11. I felt the stings on my bare legs through my running shorts and even through my T-shirt. But I was through and into the clearing. Time to get my breath. To my dismay there were no markings anywhere to be seen. All I could see, miles below me was the lone shepherd's hut. Above me I was surrounded by mountains with no discernible path. I was lost and I can honestly say I have never felt more alone.

I felt tearful and started crying - tears streaming down my face mingling with the dirt and sweat as I removed my pack and sat on a grass hummock. I wanted to give up. After all, I had managed over 250 miles. I could quit with good grace, no one had thought I would get even this far. I continued to weep head in my hands when I felt an uncomfortable biting sensation in my pants - I had sat on an ants' nest!!! I leapt up and tore off my shorts and pants and ran round in circles uncontrollably flapping at my nether regions. The tears turned to uncontrollable laughter and I know that at that moment the only way I wouldn't finish this journey was if I was in an ambulance or worse. That was the commitment that I made.

I finally got to the top and I could see the path and the village of Aneto miles and miles below. For once I decided not to do anything stupid - Aneto it was and sod the mileage.

The hotel was really nice and the staff so friendly but I was still feeling very under par and light headed - I hoped it was just a bit of sunstroke and starvation and nothing more serious. I felt a bit better after a shower and decided a big meal would sort me out.

I perused the menu pretending I could understand all the exotic dishes on offer and ordered a starter, a main and a pudding which I hoped would all be vegetarian …. I'm not convinced but I'm pretty sure whatever was served with the pasta had been living but it was delicious anyway. And a chocolate pudding is a chocolate pudding is a chocolate pudding - right!

Chapter 17

Making a plan …

"Adventure is worthwhile in itself."
Amelia Earhart

I awoke and did my customary body check to make sure all was well. I still felt a bit rough but not as bad as I had on the day before and I knew too, how important it was to stay positive.

One thing I had learnt over the years was the power of the spoken word even if it's to yourself, in fact especially to yourself. If you start telling stories about how ill you're feeling or how much your body hurts or how diffi-cult the challenge is then it can end up being self-proph-esying. It's like you're giving yourself permission to quit. I have already alluded to such moments earlier in the adventure - the boulder field, the stinging nettles to name but two.

The antidote, for me anyway, is to break things down into small chunks which when completed propel yourself resolutely towards your final goal. Social media and all too many fitness and wellbeing gurus promised you the quick fix. Well, there is no such thing in endurance running, just blood sweat and tears. Besides there were no mentors or coaches here, just myself.

I got directions from the hotel after I had hoovered up all the breakfast rolls and fruit and set out on my merry way. I wasn't quite sure where I was going to end up other than eastwards. Aneto is the highest point in the Spanish Pyrenees and I knew would be impassable for me with my set up so I was 'planning' to head further down the mountain before climbing again back up to the GR11. Progress would also be determined by how well I fared out on the trail.

The first thing was to find the path and climb out of the valley. Initially all went well but it wasn't long before the path petered out and I was sure I was going too far

South. I checked the directions from the hotel again - I had obviously missed a turning up the mountain and was just skirting the base. Yet I was sure I hadn't seen anything that looked remotely like a path. Ahead was dense undergrowth and I certainly wasn't going to head back so in the immortal words of Yazz "the only way is up". And once again I was bush wacking up the mountain through the trees and shrubbery. It was exhausting, but I knew once I got to the top I would be able to get my bearings and work out what to do.

But just as I thought I could see daylight I slipped on a moss covered log and went hurtling backwards, rolling down the mountain. I probably only slid four or five metres but it was enough to wind me and cause a really nasty cut and a spectacular bruise. I didn't get up for a few minutes but just took stock. My first thought was had I broken something? As I gingerly got up everything seemed to be moving but I had trouble putting weight on my left leg. Was this the end? A pretty ignominious way to finish - halfway up a mountain in the thick undergrowth having tripped over a log.

I massaged my leg and life started to return to it. All I had done was give myself a dead leg, a few nasty bruises, a cut and a very sore behind. A lucky escape but it had shaken me and once again my thoughts turned to how remote it was out here. But returning to what I said earlier it was essential to remain positive. This is what I had signed up for and these adversities where all part of the overall experience. After all, "got up, ran 25 miles, climbed 5,000 feet, went to bed" wouldn't make for a great experience or, come to that, a great book would it?

Finally, finally, finally after three and a half hours I found a windy track which took me to the top of the mountain and the glorious views below. Added to the views, feeling was coming back to my leg and the flies were still following me - all was well with the world. I got into the lee of the mountain and sat on a hummock (having done an 'ant check' first - yet another new routine) and surveyed the scene. I knew I should be heading further north above the Pyrenean National Park but there was no way I was going to make Espot before nightfall. I could however make Bois which was in the foot of the valley and would only take a couple of hours. I could get there by 3.00pm, patch myself up and work out my options from there. For once I had a phone signal and took that as a sign. I fired up booking.com and found a hotel - the decision was made.

The hotel was fairly unprepossessing and again I was the only guest. The owner was nice enough but I could tell that she was desperate to get back to her TV which was blaring in the other room. There was no food available so I decided to have a shower, do some washing and go and explore the delights of Bois, as for once I had arrived at a relatively civilised hour.

It was a short walk to the village and once again I was amazed at how quiet it was. The playground was empty as was the tiny supermarket and there, forming the back-drop, were the magnificent Pyrenees. One slight nagging problem was that I had come far too far down the valley and effectively had reached a dead end. But you can't tackle these sorts of problems on an empty (and rather dodgy) stomach, so I retrieved a large, two litre bottle of Aquarius, a couple of snickers bars and a brace of dough-nut-type pastries from the supermarket. I retreated to a bench by the playground and chewed thoughtfully on my 'light' snack. Something would turn up it always did - right?

I hadn't thought about Kilian for a few days but I wondered how he would approach this - probably just shoot straight over the mountain.

With my tea finished it was now time to search for some supper. There was nothing in Bois but I knew there was another village less than a mile away, perhaps I would find something there. Sure enough Evall du Bois couldn't have been more different and was absolutely buzzing with families, walkers and dogs everywhere. Cars were coming and going and I could only hear Spanish so this must be the place to come for a bit of R&R if you lived in the surrounding area. I looked at both hotel menus and decided to have a drink in one, al fresco, in the fading sun and to eat in the other. I didn't understand either menu but I would use my vegetable sign language and see where we ended up.

It was fabulous sitting outside in the sun and I was in my element - surrounded by people and activity yet completely alone. I could observe to my heart's content whilst at the same time be completely anonymous.

With the background murmur of happy chattering interspersed with laughter I took out my notebook and phone and started plotting a route to get me out of the valley. Half an hour passed and by the time the second beer had arrived I had the outline of a plan which might just work without me 'cheating' or having to go back from whence I had come. But all this plotting was making me hungry and besides it had been at least an hour since my last meal. So I settled up and moved 50 metres to the next restaurant. I got a nice table in the corner where I could study the room, study the menu and study the route I had planned and not necessarily in that order. I looked at the menu and searched hard for a pizza but to no avail - perhaps it was bit upmarket for that. I recognised the word 'rice' so I settled on that and some kind of custard tart for pudding. I don't like custard but any port in a storm as they say.

Next, I had a good look round the room. Close by there was a large table with a lot of very fit looking people on it and I realised from their T-shirts, smiling faces and general apparel they were runners and not just any old runners but part of the North Face Trail Running Team. Not so surprising, after all I had heard that this was the centre of trail running in Spain. I desperately wanted to introduce myself and tell them my story but I just couldn't pluck up the courage. Suddenly I felt very insignificant and alone. Why was it so important that people knew that I was here and that I had achieved something?

Why did I feel that I always had something to prove?
Little did I know then that the answers would come to me
over the coming weeks.

But now it was time to head back to the hotel and bed - I
had an early start. I had worked out that I could catch a
bus from the neighbouring village that would take me
due north towards Espot and back onto the GR11. I
would then dump my rucksack and run back through the
Pyrenees National Park and make up any 'east' miles that
I had gained. There was only one bus connection in the
morning so I had to pray that everything would run
smoothly and on time. But I had high hopes; after all this
was the depths of rural Spain not the UK.

I had a disturbed night involving bus fares, custard tarts
and North Face runners.

Chapter 18

A walk in the park

...

"How wild it was, to let it be."
Cheryl Strayed

I woke early. It was now time to put my master plan from last night into play. There was no brother Nick to check it over and it involved a very tight bus change. But I didn't have any choice which always makes the choice easier if you know what I mean. I had settled up with Madam the night before so I tiptoed out of the hotel and trotted the half mile to Bois and waited patiently by the bus stop. It could all go wrong at the first hurdle if the bus didn't turn up and it was ominous that I was the only person waiting for what was one of only two buses that day.

After about 20 minutes I saw a bus but it was going the wrong way. I launched myself into the middle of the road in case I was directionally challenged again (you will re-call that I had 'previous' with the Orla the dog escapade a few days back). I flapped my arms wildly and the bus screeched to a halt. "Vielha" I blurted out. The very cool driver, complete with mirrored shades, leaned out of the window and calmly said in heavily accented but perfect English; "Yes, but let me turn the bus round at the end of the village first". If he was surprised at a dishevelled, sunburnt man dressed in tattered shorts leaping out into the road and shouting at him he didn't let on.

Sure enough ten minutes later he was back. The doors swung open with a hiss and I climbed in. "Where are you going?". "Cap de Creus" I said. "That's on the Mediter-ranean coast 400km away but I can take you to Vielha where this bus finishes - that's 12km away" he smiled.

It's probably a good time (and if you have read thus far, you may have had your suspicions) to let you know that I have Aspergers. It affects people in different ways, but one of my idiosyncrasies is that I take questioning very literally so "where do you want a ticket to?" and "where are you going?" are two different things to me. But I make no excuses or apologies. In fact I look on it as a blessing that I have a set of very special gifts. Although knowing a huge number of UK postcodes, retaining conversations verbatim from years gone by or absorbing vast amounts of information from obscure topics would have limited use out here in the middle of the Pyrenees. However one of the strengths I do like to think I have is the ability to think laterally and generate novel solutions to problems ... which is just as well!

There were two other passengers on the bus; a grey haired, sprightly lady, clutching a large handbag, sitting next to a very smartly dressed Chinese lady of indeterminate age. I parked myself diagonally opposite them as they chatted away and I was soon lost in my thoughts of the what, the whys and the hows the rest of the day held in store for me. As we wound our way out of the village and started the climb to Vielha I felt a slight pang of guilt. After all I hadn't been in any form of transport since Nick had ferried me from the hotel to the various start points. But I consoled myself with the fact that I was heading due North and the few 'East' miles would be made up later in the day. And anyway, my trip my rules I reasoned.

The road was wide enough but it had no verge and I was relieved that I had decided not to try and run up it which was plan 'B'. (You will recall that less than year later I would experience some very dramatic Italian 'road running' in my attempt to run across Italy but that's another story for another day).

The grey haired lady and her companion had turned their attention to me. After all it wasn't every day that such an exotic creature graced their bus. 'Grey Hair' had already worked out that I was English from my exchange with the bus driver and couldn't contain her curiosity any longer. "Are you really going to Cap de Creus?" she asked. "Where are your belongings?". "Are you travelling alone? How old are you? Where is your wife?". When we finally arrived at Vielha I felt as though I had been through the wringer and that I had no more information to impart other than my inside leg measurement. Although come to think of it she did say I was a strange shape for a runner.

Throughout, the elegant Chinese lady had been completely silent although her gaze never left me. I guessed she didn't speak any English, but as we left the bus she turned and looked straight at me with her piercing eyes and said in perfect English; "You will succeed in your adventure but you will have a lot of trials on the way". I was lost for words, but by the time I had said my "gracias" to the bus driver they had melted into thin air. What a surreal experience coming so soon after the Orla incident and again another touch of the 'Harry Potter's'.

But I didn't have too long to reflect on it as I now had the tricky part to negotiate, the connection to Espot. Now Confucius, he say "when surrounded by buses always look for person with clipboard" and sure enough there was a nice lady with a clipboard who promised to not only get me on the right bus but even fetch me from the Café that was on the edge of the square when the bus arrived. I found a table outside and ordered a coffee and a muffin and surveyed the scene.

Most of the tables were taken up with a large group of middle aged bikers and, because it was still relatively early and the tables were littered with beer bottles, I knew they must be English. I decided to revel in my anonymity, as I often did when I was in the company of the English abroad. I can remember a time in the eighties, in the French Ski resorts, when one would never admit to being English and I would always claim to be Australian if challenged (I am actually half Australian). Although on reflection, I'm not sure that's not worse and might explain why I could never get served in the bars and restaurants.

Anyway sure enough, true to her word, Señora 'Clipboard' caught my eye and beckoned me to an awaiting bus. She helped me buy my ticket and it wasn't long before the doors hissed shut and the bus lurched out of the square and onto the road towards Espot. I studied the other passengers but there were no mysterious grey haired or Chinese ladies, just a few other happy and excited travellers with their rucksacks and walking boots ready for the next part of their adventure.

We headed East and skirted the edge of the National Park, where I would be running in an hour or two, before heading South towards Espot. In no time we arrived at this Pyrenean ski resort which is also gateway to the Aiguestores National Park. I waved goodbye to the bus driver and headed towards the hotel which I had booked the night before. Ski resorts can be strange places out of season, eerie and deserted but Espot clearly had a summer trade courtesy of the National Park with open shops and bars and there were even people too - a rarity on this journey.

The hotelier was really friendly and after he had ascertained what I was up to said he would look me up on the internet whilst I did my 'make up' miles west. He showed me some routes and said all the trails were well marked and it was nigh on impossible to get lost. But then again that was before he had looked at my website and had read about my (mis)adventures all over Europe. I emptied my rucksack in his office which must have been slightly alarming for him, filled up my water bottles and set off to find some food in the local supermarket.

It was blissful, travelling with such a light pack. It contained my running jacket, my two water bottles, some bread and cheese for my picnic, a snickers bar and a bright shiny penknife I'd bought at the ski/camping shop. I trotted out of the town and within minutes I arrived at a sign that said "Aiguestores National Park - home of trail running in the Pyrenees". The board also marked lots of different routes complete with mileages but I decided to go off piste or 'freestyle' if you prefer. After all why change the habits of a lifetime.

As I studied the board there was friendly "hola", as a lean and lithe 'Kilian' lookalike swished pass me. I decided to give him a head start, after all no point in showing him up I reasoned and by the time I had got my phone out to take a picture of him he was a speck in the distance.

I decided to follow him and I was soon in the park proper. For once, assuming I didn't get lost, I was in no rush. I had six hours to play and romp in this trail runners' paradise and I was determined to make the most of it.

The track was superb for running on - compact enough that one didn't sink in but with enough give to preserve the knees; it only needed a bit of shade to make it perfect. The temperature had been climbing and climbing over the last few days and was in the high twenties. Now I don't mind the heat, on the contrary I far prefer it to the cold, but it does mean that you have to be more mindful of the water consumption. I had already had a couple of run-ins with 'watergate' but here there would be no such problems. I had turned off the track onto a narrow path that took me into the woods and zigzagged up the mountain criss-crossing a fast flowing stream. The canopy of the trees gave me some shade and the rushing water provided the soundtrack. I was in heaven.

I hadn't seen anyone since the village until I spotted a runner descending rapidly in the distance. But this one was a bit different. As he skipped past me with a friendly nod I noticed he had a tiny child in his rucksack who could have been no more than two sleeping soundly. Well that a novel take on; "I'll just take the pram around the block to put the baby to sleep". No wonder the Spanish make such marvellous mountain athletes - they started them young.

I came to a short scree slope and stopped for some water and half a snickers. Then I had an idea. Whenever I could, I had been updating my Twitter and Facebook feeds with pictures and tales of adventure and daring. Wouldn't it be brilliant to make a little film on my iPhone and post it to Facebook and to my fan(s) back home. All the great trail runners made these short videos, normally in slow motion, of them crashing down a trail. - why not me? And so it was that the Martin Scorsese of the Pyrenees propped up his iPhone on a rock, selected slow motion and ran up to the top of the slope to begin my descent. It was as I got to the top that I realised I hadn't pressed the 'Play' button. So it was down again to the phone, press 'Play', run to the top and then run down again hopefully captured in glorious 720 frames per second. Well I would have been if the phone hadn't been dislodged in my descent and taken a video of the ground. Never mind a final attempt and success! I was pleased with my effort and would edit it this evening.

It was well past lunchtime but I was so used to not having anything to eat during the day that I decided to press on. I exited the wood into a glade with a deserted shepherd's hut and I stopped to survey the scene. Down below I could see a small dot which was Espot so I was making really good progress but I just didn't want to stop. It's quite a hard phenomenon to describe but runners do, on occasion, get into this state of euphoria where they think they can run forever and everything just seems effortless. Well now was such a moment for me and I wasn't going to waste it. I continued along the grass plateau for another half hour or so before I finally decided it was time to head back to town. I had earmarked a suitable place for my picnic with an overhanging tree right next to the stream and before long I had laid out my picnic of fresh bread and cheese with the last half of the snickers bar for pudding.

As I sat on the bank with my feet gently being massaged by the fast flowing water, my mind turned to the trials yet to come. The spectre of Andorra was now only a few days away and frankly it represented the crux of the whole adventure. I knew that I would have to run/climb well above the snow line and my equipment was totally inappropriate, but I also knew the alternative would be to head south and skirt underneath Andorra which just wasn't an option. Now you could deem this irresponsible and you would probably be right. But in every single journal I ever start (and I write every day so that's a lot) I put this quote from Helen Keller - "Life is either a daring adventure or nothing". I would mitigate the risks as much as possible, but I was determined to give it a go regardless.

I packed up the remnants of my picnic and set off down the mountain. But something had changed - the lightness of my f" of my footsteps had gone and I felt a deep melancholy settle over me. As I entered Espot I stopped at a nice but deserted bar with a terrace and I sipped an ice cold beer as the sun dipped below the mountains.

Chapter 19

Parties and fireworks

. . .

"Not until we are lost do we begin to find ourselves."

Henry David Thoreau

I awoke early and started the morning rituals - spectacles, …. You know the routine by now. I'd had a nice chat with the hotelier the night before and he confirmed that yes, there was still snow on the route into Andorra but it was getting warmer and warmer. I could vouch for that after my adventures in the park that afternoon but we both agreed there was no alternative route. The GR11 is the GR11 is the GR11 and it wasn't going to be changed overnight because one decrepit Englishman was worried about getting his feet wet.

The hotel was deserted as I crept out onto the street and the first thing I could see was the moon over the mountains although dawn had already broken - a good start. I had to do three stages today which give or take would be another marathon and an elevation gain of over 8,000ft.

Brian Johnson's excellent GR11 Trail guide had cheerfully informed me too, that this was the easiest place to get lost on the GR11 and somehow, I just knew that I wasn't going to disappoint. But never mind you know the mantra - onwards and upwards and travel hopefully.

Every single moment on this trip was magical and enlivening, even when I faced danger (the ice wall springs to mind), but there was something special about the moment before I took the first step of the day. It was a step into the unknown in the most literal way - I just had no idea who or what I was going to encounter and I suppose this lack of control is what made it both exciting and terrifying at the same time. This was so alien to me. Usually any lack of control or uncertainty totally freaked me out to the extent that I would watch the same film again and again safe in the knowledge that I knew the outcome or I would watch a replay of a rugby match after it had ended safe in the knowledge that I knew result. I don't really read much fiction probably because I have to read the end first to make sure there are no surprises. I guess this rather defeats the author's intentions, particularly if it is a mystery and suspense novel. By the way feel free to go to the last page of this book to see if 'he did or he didn't' - I quite understand. There were some exceptions - I used to ski off bars quite regularly as well as down the stairs of my house in Wimbledon but there was probably some-thing else behind that, not least copious quantities of al-cohol. Anyway back to the control dynamic; perhaps I had stumbled onto a revolutionary cure for my affliction - launch yourself off into the mountain with no compass or map, inadequate supplies of food and water and make sure you're inappropriately clothed too and just see what happens. Hmm ... go figure.

Anyway enough rambling and time to take that first step. I trotted off down the street and before long saw the fa-miliar GR11 chevrons and a well made up track that would take me towards Iou. I was wearing a second layer but I knew it wouldn't be long before I would be stripping off - today was going to be a scorcher just as I had been promised. I crossed onto a steep path that cut out the switchbacks of the track and then it contoured the valley before starting the descent to Jou.

The legs were moving easily from my jaunt yesterday and in less than 90 minutes I had completed stage 1 and was so pleased with myself that I decided to have a little coffee and muffin at the small pit stop. I knew it was going to be harder from here on in for, as I alluded to earlier, Mr Johnson told me so:

"It is worth making an early start on this stage as the long steep ascent could be very tiring in the full heat of the day. It is also worth carrying plenty of water from Dorve. This is the stage on the GR11 where you are most likely to lose the route so pay careful attention to your navigation."

I passed the most fabulous lake, crystal clear and with the backdrop of the mountains perfectly projected in the reflection. I stopped to take a few photos on my phone - I could always look at them later when the water ran out. Along the side of the lake there were these peculiar man-made constructions which I later discovered were machine gun nests built as part of Franco's Pyrenean defence line. Not just an adventure story this; stick with me and you'll learn something new every day.

I pressed on, climbing up and up, through yet another deserted and derelict hamlet where mercifully there was a water point. This time I made sure that the bottles were full and my thirst has been slaked. This was it, as far as water was concerned, until the end of the stage. The way markings were pretty sporadic and it wasn't long before I was completely lost again. My progress slowed to a crawl as I circled around like an ant trying to find his way out of a jar. But the Marco Polo of the Spanish Pyrenees was by now a master of navigation and I whipped out my phone and fired up google maps. There was a large blue blob on the screen but by inching forward I could see the direction I was travelling in and surprise surprise I was heading the right way. I took a bearing and checked every 30 minutes or so that I was still on track. The approach to the Coll took me through an enchanted wood with the sun streaming through the trees creating mottled patterns on the weary traveller below. Through a high meadow and then I was on the ridge, covered in a blanket of yellow gorse with the Pyrenees stretching as far as the eye could see. There was just me and the mountains, both playing a part in this fantastic story.

I started the descent down a steep and exposed path desperately seeking water. I crossed a tiny stream that was barely more than a puddle. I didn't even think twice about it - I filled my bottles and drank and drank trusting that my Masai upbringing and a cast-iron stomach would protect me from any contaminants.

The path was so narrow and the drop so severe that it was like running on the edge of the world but on an on I went before the terrain levelled out and the path became wider. But my adventures weren't over - there was a lot of shouting and screeching to my right and suddenly a wild boar came crashing out of the thicket onto the path a few feet in front of me before haring off down the path. It must be a hunt and I prayed that the shouting didn't turn to shooting as I ran as fast as my tired legs would carry me after the boar.

I was rewarded with another spectacular open air traverse before the final descent as dusk descended on the village of Tavascan and what I hoped would be sanctuary. It was the night of the EU referendum and Taviscan was in party mood.

The hotel was absolutely fabulous and the receptionist so friendly - she even forgave me for being English on this night of all nights. I explored the town and had a beer and something to eat before returning to the hotel and the comfort of my bed. I fell asleep to the sound of happy revellers and fireworks at midnight. What a day and just one more to go before Andorra.

Chapter 20

Snakes and switchbacks …

"Adventure is worthwhile."

Aesop

I really didn't want to leave the hotel - they had been so nice and helpful even to the point of ringing a friend of theirs at my next stop-off point, Aruel, and sorting out a room for me.

Today should be an easy day (how many times had I said that to myself on this trip) with about 25 km and 5,000 feet of ascent - a mere bagatelle.

Now if you're a runner, and I'm guessing you must have at least some interest in the subject to have got this far, you will know that there are two schools of thought regarding stretching before setting out on your run. There is the 'Dynamic' school who advocate an enormously complicated and lengthy routine with side lunges, back lunges and every other type of lunge you could possibly think of and quite frankly leaves you exhausted before you've even set out. Then there is the 'Kilian' method which involves grasping your foot as you kick it back up towards your butt a couple of times (preferably while updating social media, reading a map, checking your gear, etc) then off. Naturally I favour a variation of the latter or the 'Kilian Lite' if you will. This involves touching your knees with your hands once and then you're good to go.

Today I felt stiff as a board and even though the hour was early it was already hot. But how could you possibly not be motivated in these beautiful mountains and sure enough soon after starting out, the joints and bones warmed up and I got into a steady rhythm on the gentle undulating path. I passed a huge orange and blue banner proclaiming 'Fets Catalunya'. This was actually more exciting than it sounds. Catalonia or Catalunya to give it its original spelling was the last region on the journey. I had already run across Galicia, Asturias, Cantabra, Basque Country, Navarra, and Aragon which just left Catalunya to go. Obviously there was the small matter of Andorra to negotiate but that was but a blimp on life's highway I reassured myself.

The path got steeper and narrower and ahead I saw two hikers, their laughter and happy voices carrying down the path spurring me on. I caught them up and we had a brief exchange. They were young and of course spoke perfect English. They were taking a break from the city and where better than the Pyrenees to get away from it all. And "where are you going?" they asked. When I told them they were suitably amazed but were more interested in the mechanics of it and my total lack of gear - perhaps they had ideas for a future adventure too! I was feeling good so I waved my goodbyes and pressed on.

A green snake slithered across the path in front of me which not only gave me a start but reminded me how hot it was. It was already in the 30s and the water was perilously low. By now I was used to not having food during the day but the water was another matter and the lack of it was always in the back of my mind. The 'path' such as it was started to traverse along the side of the mountain and once again, I was subjected to Health and Safety

Pyrenean style. There were metal wires forming a sort of bannister along the side of the cliff face which you hung onto as you edged your way along with a shear drop inches from your feet. I had to take pictures - surely no one would believe this; so with one arm hooked around the wire support and the other clutching my phone I snapped away for posterity. Definitely another one for the memoirs.

The traverse ended and the path returned to normal, eventually leading to a picturesque yet deserted village. Where was everyone? Then I remembered a little song from my childhood "only mad dogs and Englishmen go out in the midday sun". I came to a trough with an old rusty pipe dripping water into it. Above it was a sign the gist of which I now recognised as "don't drink the water". Any port in a storm I thought as I drank and drank and filled up my two bottles as well. This could be a real test for the 'Masai stomach' - let's see.

I found the markings and left the village up a steep, winding track with one switchback after another. It was too steep to try and cut the corners and besides I had already tried that tactic a few days previously with disastrous consequences (you'll remember the big fall and the bush wacking escapade). Just remember the mantra "one foot in front of the other".

After what seemed like an age I looked back to check on my progress and was dismayed to see that the village didn't seem to be getting any smaller in fact if anything it looked bigger. So that's why they tell you to never look back.

But I did finally get to the top and just as the day before, there was a carpet of yellow gorse as far as the eye could see and there, in the distance, were the snow capped mountains leading to Andorra. But I didn't dawdle - it had already taken me an hour longer than I had expected and I could see that despite or maybe because of the heat, the storm clouds were gathering on the horizon.

I pressed on through a thicket all the while surrounded by bright yellow before I was greeted by an extraordinary sight. No not wild boar, dogs, bears or snakes but a VW camper van. It was completely incongruous stuck out here in the middle of nowhere and how did it get here? I hadn't seen anyone since the hikers this morning - maybe another touch of the 'Harry Potter's'. I passed it swiftly but there was no one about and I started the long descent towards Aruel. Needless to say I had run out of water again but if the thunder and lightning didn't get me, then at least I wouldn't be thirsty.

The little hotel was lovely - I knew it would be if they were friends of the people from the day before. With perfect timing and just as I got to my room and stuck my head under the tap the heavens opened. I decided to go straight out and see if I could forage something to eat and then I would come back, shower and change before dinner. Who was I kidding, put a less dirty T-shirt on more like.

I found a little bar and I like to think I did my little bit to promote the Brits after the referendum result. Anyway the lady behind the bar was very impressed with my order for three Aquarius, one tea, one ice cream, a beer and a muffin. Excellent, now time to go and find something for supper.

Chapter 21

Race to Andorra …

"Life is either daring adventure or nothing at all."

Helen Keller

I woke just after 5.00am – no alarm needed, my aches and pains providing the necessary wake up call. A quick shower and with teeth brushed I was ready for the next onerous task of the day – trying to find some clean running gear or perhaps I should say the least dirty!

So I had finally arrived at <u>the</u> day, the day that I was going to cross the border and leave Spain behind, albeit briefly, and cross into Andorra. I had imagined this to be the crux of the whole trip - if I had success here then I would have a good chance of getting to Cap de Creus and the fabled lighthouse. Fail and I would be on the next flight home ... or worse. I have to be honest and admit that I had been advised not to go via this route with my limited gear both from locals and from interested parties back in the UK. I hadn't actually admitted to anyone what I was doing but then (as you now know) I am a man of few words and most of those mumbled at that.

But enough fanning about - time to be decisive and get the game face on … again. A couple of 'Kilian stretches' and I was off.

I crossed the river and started climbing through the woods before I reached the open meadows. My feet were already wet from following the waterlogged track caused by last night's storm. This didn't bode well for the long day ahead. It was getting hot and I had long since stripped off my running jacket and was in the obligatory shorts and tee. Sure enough, all this prevaricating and analysing had made me lose concentration and I was lost.

Fortunately I didn't have too far to descend before I picked up the familiar red and white markings of the GR11 La Senda trail again. The terrain was relatively flat for a mile or so and I was able to pick up the pace which was just as well as I knew that today would probably be the most testing to-date. After all I was climbing to 2,700 metres before descending into Andorra.

It wasn't long before the lush meadows gave way to more woods and a steep path wending its way ever upwards. I was just congratulating myself on my progress when the inevitable happened. I had faced so many fears already on this trip – unruly cows, rabid farm dogs, snakes and even wild boar, getting lost, running out of water. But what I feared most was a big fall. Where I was running was so remote and sometimes I would go through the whole day with only seeing one or two people. I was negotiating a particularly rocky part of the path crossing over a fallen tree when my foot caught a root and I did a not so graceful face plant. I didn't get up straight away but took stock – everything still working just a few scratches and dented pride. As I picked myself up something caught my eye and there glinting in the sunshine was a brand new pair of Rayban sunglasses. How incongruous – I hadn't seen anyone since the night before and here were these glasses waiting for me. I felt guilty about picking them up but it would be crazy just to leave them I justified to myself!

Another hour saw me reach a plateau with a rough car park where the not so intrepid could drive to, have a picnic and explore the fabulous scenery. People! This was a new phenomenon for me. As I left the car park I bumped into a couple of young hikers who asked me the way towards Andorra. I was always amused when people asked me the way – I supposed I looked like I knew what I was doing with my running stuff and rucksack and, after all, what madman would be crossing the Pyrenees without having planned a proper route! It transpired they were from Madrid but working in Milton Keynes … still I suppose everyone has their cross to bear. Anyway we parted company as I broke into a trot on the relatively flat valley floor; I was conscious that time was moving on and I had the big climb ahead.

The trail was hard to pick up through the boulder field but I kept looking for little cairns that kept me on track. The snow too was now more evident and my heart sank when I saw two people coming towards me in full mountain gear, jackets, coats and crampons and ice axes attached to their rucksacks. They were lost and French (not that that is mutually exclusive and I would know). I was able to reassure them that they were on the right track and probably four or five hours from their destination. They asked where I was going and when I replied "Andorra" they looked at me in my running shorts, running shoes, T-shirt and lightweight running jacket then at each other. "I think you ought to turn back, there is snow up to your waist in some parts and you just don't have the right gear".

I knew finally it was decision time and despite all my brave words to myself this morning I had one more chance. Everyone had told me that I would struggle on this section without the proper equipment but the thought of heading five hours back to where I started from was soul destroying and besides where would I go from there? Somehow, despite all the warnings I knew that I would be safe and I also knew that my decision now would define the rest of the adventure. Succeed and it would give me so much confidence for the arduous days ahead. I thanked them and said that I was going to press on and set off without looking back – would I come to regret this decision?

As I climbed the temperature dropped dramatically and

the patches of snow became larger and larger. It was not possible to skirt around them so I followed the footsteps in the snow, ominously, they were all pointing downwards and not upwards. I was a keen skier so I knew that snow wasn't always as it seemed. One minute you could be walking on a crust and the next sunk up to your waist.

I was trying to get to a refuge that was perched precariously on top of a large ledge secured to the rock with wires to avoid blowing off. The picture in the guide showed it as being manufactured in aluminium, almost like a fifties American diner. But it was one thing looking at the picture in a book but trying to find it was another matter and then out of the corner of my eye I saw the metal refuge glinting in the sun and my spirits rose.

I had to do a little bit of rock climbing onto the ledge and there, to my surprise, I saw a man sitting on the steps of the refuge eating a cake. We introduced ourselves and I looked longingly at the cake. I hadn't eaten anything since the night before other than a bit of congealed, melted chocolate that I had found in one of the rucksack pockets and I was famished but not famished enough to ask my new friend for a piece of cake – oh the British reserve!

But the good news was that he had come over from Andorra and that the route was possible although the next bit would be tricky without proper mountain boots. It had taken him six hours so it looked like I would be doing the last bit in the dark but there was nothing else than to go for it! I set off through the snow, running shoes and socks by now soaking wet, and skirted round a lake before ascending a very steep path. This led to a snow field up the side of the mountain which would be followed by what looked like an almost sheer scree and boulder face to the summit. My German friend from the refuge had explained that, mathematically the scree was unlikely to crush me because the angle was just within the limit before it would fall – great!

From the base of the snow wall I looked up several hundred metres to the final scree slope and the summit. It looked impossible but it was now or never and I took my first tentative step. I tried to plot a course between boulders to minimise the amount that I would fall if the worst happened and I knew, from my previous mountain experience several decades earlier, that it was just a case of going slowly and always trying to have three limbs on the mountain. I kicked into the snow with my running shoes to create a step and gradually wended my way up the slope. As I got to the first refuge point, a group of protruding rocks, I sank into the snow up to my waist but I hauled myself up onto the rocks and took stock. I saw my course – maybe four more 'rock stops' and I would be at the foot of the scree slope, this was on! I was wet, cold and bedraggled but getting to the top would give me all the lift I needed and I could change clothes at the top.

Thirty minutes later and I was at the foot of the scree slope and the final ascent. I decided to go as fast as I could - forget taking it easy. I had to keep moving in case the scree started to go. A final sip of water and a gear check and I was off. I was on all fours scrambling as fast as I could, sweat pouring off me despite the cold and wind. I edged towards the side of the slope to hang onto a rock for a breather and then the final few metres before I was at the brow and over the other side. I tore off my rucksack and gave a scream for joy and did a little victory dance too. After all there was no YouTube up here. I had done it, 2,700 metres and before me was Andorra, an other huge milestone in my journey.

I took a few pictures, changed socks and T- shirt and started the descent to Andorra where a bath, food and a warm bed awaited me. The scenery was spectacular – I descended a steep path and made my way down another small snow field entering a 'Shangrilaesque' hanging valley where I passed between two lakes.

Here I came across two young hikers who looked suitably amazed when I ran past them. I stopped for a rest on a boulder further down where they caught me up and a little competition ensued! I really should know better at my age but these 20-year-olds, fully kitted with their poles and mountain boots, didn't like been overtaken by the old timer and English at that! Off we went haring down the slope, they were just in front but then they took a wrong turning and I regained the lead. Down, down hurtling along the narrow path, all tiredness and hunger forgotten in the push for victory.

Then the inevitable happened and my ego and the young hikers caught me at the same time as I tripped on a stone trying to leap across a narrow stream, went flying and landed in a crumpled heap on the path, sunglasses and hat jettisoned in the fall. They passed me without a glance, let alone a word to find out if I was OK. The race wasn't over! I picked myself up, a few cuts and bruises, nothing serious and hared after them – we reached the tarmac path as one and I knew I had them – they were tiring and nothing was going to stop me now. I pulled away and before long, just as the last rays of the day were disappearing behind the mountains, I was on the outskirts of Arinsal.

I found a grubby bar that was open and feasted on peanuts and lemonade. The clientele consisted of a maudlin Englishman who looked like he'd been left here at the end of the ski season by his mates and a grumpy barman who never took his eyes off his phone screen even whilst using the till. I got onto Booking.com and looked for a hotel. They all looked fairy grim but I plumped on the one with the best'ish reviews and would take my chances. I had been in Andorra once as a fresh faced 18-year-old having just left school to travel around Europe. I had got drunk on duty free spirits the entire time I was here which was only 24 hours and I do vaguely remember buying a car - a very old Simca Aronde which in the end, took me all the way to Amsterdam and back. Ahh happy days.

But I digress. I think you'll know by now that I'm not a big winger in the grand scope of things but the hotel does deserve a mention in dispatches. Me and the ever increasingly embarrassed receptionist tried five rooms before we found one where the bed had been made up and there weren't piles of rubbish everywhere. But I tried to make light of it - no point in making the young girl feel more awkward than she already did and the sixth room was more or less OK - the bed was made up anyway.

I had a shower, a bit of 'Masai washing' and now it was time to hit the hot spots of Arinsal and find some of that duty free spirit to deaden the pain of being back in civilisation. Oh how I longed for my mountains.

Chapter 22

The Navigator …

"Only one who wanders finds new paths."
Norwegian Proverb

I was so pleased to be leaving Arinsal but there were other reasons for having an extra skip in my step today. It's time to introduce you to another character in this adventure - my sister Jojo. She had decided to join me for the last leg of the adventure, the final push to the Mediterranean. So you've already met my brother and sister-in-law, how can I best describe my sister. Well, I think intrepid is probably the best word. She had climbed Kilimanjaro with my brother in her twenties and never really looked back. She is an inveterate explorer and traveller and walks everywhere always carrying her portmanteau, a treasure trove of insect repellent, maps, torches, energy bars, insurance documents, her will, banks statements, phone chargers, iPads, keys to properties long since departed, etc. I think you get the picture. It weighs a ton but doesn't seem to trouble her at all - it's just part of her everyday attire. Sometimes she accompanies me on my more exotic races in Spain and of course charms everyone she meets. Often to be seen in the front of the race director's car, clutching her portmanteau and ready to be taken to the next checkpoint - quite the celebrity!

But ... there is always a but isn't there. She has a dark secret. Despite being an avid collector of maps, she has, without doubt, the worse sense of direction of anyone that I have ever met. She will even resort to phoning my brother thousands of miles away (who as you know has a brilliant sense of direction), for directions to a hotel or village. On more than one occasion he's had to 'talk her in' like an air traffic controller and a stricken plane. How on earth was she going to get from Barcelona, where she had never been, in a country she had never driven in, in a car she had never seen, across a border completely alone to a hotel in the middle of a large Andorran town. I somehow had a feeling she would manage it!

I left the hotel and was soon running down a steep hill, across a stream and to the foot of the forest. I pressed on making the most of the relatively flat terrain. A short climb and a little descent to the village of Arans. I glanced at my watch - under three hours. I was ahead of schedule and the next stop was the rendezvous in the town of Encamp. I left the village and soon the road petered out into a track which in turn petered out into a path and a steep one at that.

I knew that there was a lot more climbing to do before the final descent to Encamp which, if all went well, would be about four hours away. I retreated into my bubble and the ultra runners mantra "one foot in front of the other, one foot in front of the other". Isn't it funny (and a mistake) how we can judge a whole country and all it's inhabitants on one's first impression. I'd had my nose put out of joint by the 'race' with the unsympathetic hikers, the disinterested barman and the grubby hotel. And as a result the whole of Andorra was judged by the same token - another lesson in life for my notebook.

I resolved to make the most of Encamp and be nice to everyone if and when I arrived. I reached a very high picnic spot where there was a family with kids playing and enjoying the sunshine. Now was my chance, but my reserve took over and I slunk off to a corner to sit down and rest. The father came over and offered me water and something to eat from his picnic. I was so touched - me a complete stranger and a pretty bedraggled one at that. A sort of poor man's wild man of Borneo look. I gratefully accepted the water but declined the food and we had a chat. It was a Sunday (I had long forgotten the days of the week by now) and he had bought his family out for a picnic and an outing in the woods. My very own "Aquarius" filled up my bottles and we said our goodbyes, him smiling, and me suitably chastened about my jaundiced view I had had of Andorra and Andorrans in general on my arrival.

I finally got to the ridge and started the long descent into Encamp. Long before I reached the town I could hear the sounds of cars revving up and screeching and a very loud tannoy system blaring out commentary and music in equal quantities. Remembering my earlier sermon I said through gritted teeth "I'm going to love this place!".

But I was finally here and now to find the rendezvous point and my sister although I suspected she was probably in Gibraltar by now.

But there, to my amazement, wearing bright pink shorts and espadrilles coming through the swing doors was Jojo.

"Hello I haven't been here long, the drive was fine. I'm glad you found the hotel all right". I had visions of a trail of destruction from Barcelona Airport with bicycles and pedestrians climbing lamp posts, grannies leaping off the side walks, cars bumping into each other and buses desperately back pedalling down bus lanes as they were approached by a little speeding VW. And all the while the portmanteau spilling its contents onto the front seat with a trail of wires and chargers. But still I was very pleased to see her and I kept my vision to myself. "Have you got any food?" I ventured.

We were across the border in minutes and back into Spain. We had hired an apartment in a little complex on the outskirts of La Seu d'Urgell and this would be our base for the next few days as I ventured ever further east towards the Mediterranean. As we drove Jojo told me about her adventure from Barcelona Airport.

Now to set the scene, she had never owned a smart phone until the day before she flew, so the navigational properties of such a beast would probably be beyond her until I had given her a crash course. She had arrived at the car hire desk where they had decided, on the spur of the moment, to give her an upgrade to a car that included Satnav. She smiled sweetly and told them that she had never used Satnav so the manager had taken her personally to the car, reprogrammed the Satnav for English and punched in "Encamp". She handed her the keys pressed start on the Satnav and waved her off. She had then driven through Barcelona, along the motorway and across the border into Andorra and then driven to the hotel and parked outside in the one remaining space. This is how her world rocks!

The apartment was one of half a dozen or so that surrounded a stone flagged quadrangle in the middle of which sat a large cat which, to my knowledge, never moved the entire time we were there even when some of the other residents had an impromptu birthday party around it. The owner was such fun and very interested in my adventure. It transpired that Kilian's mother, the formidable Nuria, was a friend of hers so a slightly tenuous connection to my hero but I would take it.

A bit of 'Masai washing' and then it was time to paint La Seu d'Urgell red and find something to eat.

La Seu d'Urgell was a really lively town - the whole world and his aunt were out, with ages ranging from two months to 90+, and everyone seemed to mix seamlessly. There was a complete lack of tension which I always felt back home when I was out 'after hours' and I'd certainly felt in Andorra. We found a couple of seats in a busy bar and ordered some tapas, a vino rosado for the navigator and a beer for me. The tapas was delicious and the potato croquettes to die for. We made friends with the waiter and promised we would be back the following night.

We got back to the apartment and Jojo got out all her maps to 'plot' tomorrow's route … and I went to bed.

Chapter 23

The Gangster …

"Live, travel, adventure, bless and don't be sorry."

Jack Kerouac

A fter the trials of Andorra I was planning a relatively quiet day today with about 23 miles of running and 2,500 ft of ascent. My pack would be super light with a spare top, water, phone and that rarest of commodities food courtesy of Jojo and the portmanteau which was a treasure trove of goodies for the hungry runner.

But first things first. I had the luxury of a later start which meant just one thing … no not a lie in, but breakfast! Now you may think this is the simplest meal of the day but not in Cal Miguel it wasn't. It transpired you needed to be an expert in mathematics and logistical planning. The kitchen was a short distance across the quadrangle which was just as well. The kettle was in the kitchen but the water wasn't, so this entailed a run across the quad and up the stairs to the apartment clutching the kettle. Next a quick fill of the kettle in the sink and back across the quad to the kitchen. Each guest was presented with a chart with a tariff of prices. So one yoghurt = 1 euro, a slice of bread 50 cents which sounds fine but when you got down to a knob of butter at 50 cents and a dollop of jam well - what constituted a knob (don't answer that) and what constituted a dollop? But no time to fret about that as it was another mad dash across the quad for more water.

Anyway breakfast finished it was time for Jojo to drop me off at Josa de Cadi which was due South of Encamp and my starting point for the day. We parked the car and poured over a map working out the rendezvous point for the end of the day. I don't know why we bothered, neither of us could read it properly but we went through the motions umming and ahhing and nodding sagely. After all, at the end of the day, brother Nick back in mission control, Devon could talk us in.

191

I set off along a narrow road through the centre of the panoramic valley, relishing life with the lighter pack. Pitter patter, pitter patter my shoes slapped out a steady rhythm on the tarmac. I'd better make the most of this, if all went well I would be back on the more testing terrain of the GR11 by tomorrow and the final push towards the coast.

Was it really possible that I was going to follow in the footsteps of Kilian and finish this epic adventure? But I knew by now that "there is many a slip betwixt cup and lip" and I was entering the most dangerous phase of the trip. I had been incredibly lucky with injuries but, If I'm honest, everything ached and the constant dehydration and lack of food during the day was taking it's toll. I was aware too, that an injury could be just around the corner. On the other hand it might not and that was the attitude I chose to adopt.

I turned off the road onto a well worn track. I was sharing the path and the surrounding meadows with a flock of sheep and a lone shepherd and his dog. He could have been from central casting (that's the shepherd not the dog). Rugged, good looking and leaning on a shepherd's

crook while his dog sat patiently at his side. He had a
battered little rucksack and the romantic in me liked to
imagine it had a hunk of homemade bread and some
cheese from the farm in it together with a bottle of strong
red wine (although it probably contained a couple of
snickers and a can of red bull). He looked so at peace
with the world that I skirted around him so as not to disturb his reverie. I wonder what he thought about out here
all alone every day. Probably not about life on social media and how to stand out in the world like the vast majority of us. I saw him again from a distance 45 minutes
later, after a brief wrong turning and a little sojourn into
the undergrowth, and I swear he hadn't moved a muscle.

Enough romanticising I had work to do. I found the correct turn off and went along a very narrow path with a
spectacular drop on one side into the gorge below. In theory I only had about ten miles to the rendezvous but
something didn't seem quite right. I came across a herd of
goats, little bells sending a cacophony of noise out into
the wilderness. I wasn't sure what the danger quotient
was with goats vis a vis wild boar, rabid dogs and snakes
but they seemed totally disinterested in me and more con
cerned with the lush grass. Next, I came to a roped off
area with a sign that my rudimentary Spanish told me

said, "beware of the bees", although if I'm honest the hives were a bit of a giveaway. But the path just seemed to have petered out and I was starting to go down the side of the valley through ever thicker greenery and before long I was back to my favourite pastime, bush whacking. By now I was getting used to this and I would normally have taken it in my stride but today, for some reason it really got to me, and I yelled in frustration smacking wildly at the bushes with my fists.

I calmed myself down and started climbing up through the undergrowth to the ridge to get my bearings. But to my horror it looked like I had managed to get myself into someone's private garden. But not any old garden. There were security cameras everywhere and I had visions of black clad guards and snarling Alsatians appearing at any moment to apprehend me. So I did what any directionally challenged sexagenarian would do - that's right I legged it up the drive as fast as I could.

The drive gave way to a single track road which is turn led to the village of Macaners. I'd had enough and slumped down on the edge of the road exhausted, using the sign post as a back support. As I had predicted earlier in the day, I was starting to struggle and not just physically but more importantly mentally too. I checked my watch - I had done just over 20 miles and climbed a few thousand feet. It would mean a longer day tomorrow but if I packed up now at least there would be a tomorrow and another chance to try and conquer this feat and my demons too. No, my mind was made up I called Jojo who thankfully had a signal and we arranged to meet up.

I don't know what I was whining about but I'd had a deeply demoralising day and felt despondent. I'd better get my act together before Jojo arrived – she didn't 'do' despondent.

Sure enough, she was her normal happy self, so much so that we decided to stop for a drink on the way back before getting into our glad rags to keep our promise with the waiter from the night before. It's amazing how some people can just uplift you however tired you feel and I was smiling like a Cheshire cat by the time I left the tapas bar. Although, on reflection, it might have had something to do with the glass of Rioja I had to accompany the potato croquettes and ice cold beer.

Chapter 24

Cornfields and electric fences …

"Getting lost is sometimes the best way to find yourself."

Maxime Lagace

I awoke afresh and felt a lot better than the day before. Today was an exciting day (what day wasn't) as, if all went to plan, I would be passing through Kilian's home town, Puiguicerda. Who knows I might even bump into the great man and he might want to run a few miles with me. But before all that there was the thrill and the mental power games with the 'breakfast run' - how many times would I need to go back to the apartment clutching the kettle this time?

Breakfast completed Jojo dropped me off at the previous days stopping point and off I went. I would have to add on the 'missing miles' from last night and I knew there was a lot of climbing today, but I was in a completely different frame of mind and was up for it. It really is amazing the power that the mind has over the body and running above all other sports proves the connection between the two - mind and body. It's completely indiscriminate too. You can be a highly tuned athlete but one setback and the mind starts playing games and you can become an 'also ran' in the blink of an eye. Conversely, as I've alluded to before, you can be like me — the body completely trashed but you don't give pain a voice, you break down each part of the challenge into manageable chunks, from tree to tree, from peak to peak and you can overcome pretty much everything. I've seen this played out so many times on really long endurance races which are a real lesson in human nature (as well as an eating competition with a run chucked in).

The first part was flat and before long I was running past large, opulent houses on the outskirts of Puigicerda. It was very different from the rustic idyll I had experienced up to now. I had arranged to meet Jojo for a coffee and some calories in the town centre and somehow this went without a hitch. Jojo had even had time to buy me a beautiful, bright red Salomon cap to replace the one that had gone missing after my epic fall during the race on the descent to Andorra. A coffee and a snickers later and I was on my way. I was conscious that I had a long way to go and all the climbing was loaded into the back end of the day.

On the outskirts of Puigicerda I saw a beautiful runner coming towards me. She ran like a gazelle compared to my heavy footed elephant steps. But despite the 420 miles and 90,000 feet of elevation that proceeded me I managed to get into 'Strutting Peacock Mode' one more time. This involves pulling your tummy in, running bolt upright and on the balls of your feet with hardly any breathing at all. It's all a question of timing - I can keep this up for about 12 seconds before everything collapses and hangs out. Next time you're running in the park have a look and see if you can spot a proponent of 'Strutting Peacock Mode' - we're everywhere and it normally proceeds a huge fall as the unnatural pose lends itself to a propensity for tripping. But we are all part of the same community and, as if to prove that, the girl gave me a huge smile as we said our "Holas" and crossed paths. If that smile wouldn't get me to the top of the mountain then nothing would.

Incidentally, as an aside, you can attempt 'SPM' when skiing. This involves lurking on the side of the piste just above the crowded mountain restaurant and then when the time is right launching yourself down the slope, legs tightly together with not a chink of light between them. Obviously you can't turn properly but you only need to put one final turn in, finishing with a huge plume of snow just by the restaurant. But be warned this can have dis-astrous results - the secret is in finding exactly the right place to launch from, commensurate with your skiing standards (which in my case are appalling). Set off too low and you arrive at the restaurant like a damp squib which won't impress the lunchtime revellers at all and too high well ... many is the time when I've had to abort the stop, hurtling past the restaurant at near terminal velo-city to have a stupendous crash lower down. But as long as you're out of sight of the restaurant it's all good and you can blame it on a sticky binding if anyone tries to come and rescue you

I saw the turning for the path I was meant to take but it

struck me that a shortcut across a cornfield would save me some time and negate some climbing. After all no point in doing three sides of the triangle - right. An hour later I was circling aimlessly in this enormous cornfield like a cartoon character in a Disney film. I finally found my way out with the help of Google maps but my demeanour wasn't improved when I got my giblets caught trying to straddle an electric fence and in case you're wondering - yes, it was on.

I doubled back and joined the path and started the long, inexorable climb. Finally after a gut busting few hours I got to the top and along the ridge which borders France and Spain. I saw the way markers which I hadn't seen for days and it reminded me of what I was trying to do. More excitement as I had to run though a herd of cows grazing happily on the ridge. But somehow my fears of the cows had dissipated although it had taken 22 days for me to achieve this state. However, there was no time to congratulate myself as the tanks were dry - I'd long since run out of water and I had a blinding headache with the effects of dehydration and the long climb. As I made the descent I came across a stream - it was barely more than a trickle and clearly unsafe with cows just a few hundred metres above it. But who cares. I drank and drank and drank before continuing the descent. I slipped and slid down the mountain at an alarming rate barely having time to take in the remarkable sight of a man asleep in the middle of a flock of sheep. (Well I hope he was asleep).

I finally got to Planoles exhausted. But there was the navigator and quartermaster with copious quantities of ice cream and Aquarius. And guess what? She had made friends with the 'Grand Fromage' of Planoles who had assured her that this was his town and she could have anything she wanted. Maybe he was the man with the large Range Rover whose garden I had run through yesterday. On reflection he did look at me a bit sideways when we were introduced.

We returned to the apartment where they were having an impromptu birthday party in the quad with happy kids laughing and playing all observed, of course, by the cat who hadn't moved a muscle.

I was tired but happy and we had a date to keep with our barman in La Seu d'Urgell. It was our last night here so we were going to have a drink with him and then maybe something else other than the croquettes. Perhaps something really sophisticated like a pizza.

We had a drink with our friend and then headed to the main square for our pizza. We found a place where we could sit outside in the warm balmy evening and it was heaven. Happy, fun loving people from every generation enjoying a night out and their joy was infectious. You've got to be happy in life. First and foremost because there's no point in being any other way and secondly because, well … it pisses people off.

But all was not unbridled joy. No. We had a major problem - we had run out of soap and that meant no 'Masai washing' and in fact no washing of any sort. "Have another glass of wine and leave it with me", Jojo announced before leaping from the table with her portmanteau and through the enormous gates of a very posh hotel opposite. Ten minutes later she re-appeared clutching the portmanteau from which spilled a small bottle of Evian containing a few squirts of the finest hotel soap. The story unfolded … she had gone to the reception desk and said that she was considering staying there in the future, what were their best rates. She has a certain presence my sister and after they gave her their very best rates and offered to show her around, she announced that she didn't need to see the rooms but whilst she was here could she use the loos. The rest is history and that's the story of the soap and how this runner smelt pretty great even after 525 miles.

We returned to the apartment for the last time - they were still partying but nothing was going to stop me from sleeping and I was asleep as my head touched the pillow tired but elated and ready for whatever the last days could throw at me. Little did I know what lay ahead.

Chapter 25

Hollywood calling

. . .

"Every time you are willing to say "Yes" to everything on your path, you express the hero inside of you."

Maria Nemeth

The next morning we packed up early before saying our goodbyes to the Señora and of course the cat. I'd had some real adventures here over the last couple of days but I was ready to move on to pastures new and to see what life had in store for me.

The clouds looked ominous as I was dropped at the start point but this only served to enhance the mountains and the cracked terracotta roofs of the dilapidated farm buildings on the side of the track. Rain was definitely in the air.

Sure enough, I'd only gone a mile or two, before the heavens opened. I donned my rain jacket for one of the very few times on the trip and the zip promptly bust. I hoped this 'easy' day wasn't going to turn into one of 'those' days. I was a bit upset about the zip but most of my gear was held together with safety pins and actually it was rather nice splashing through the rain after the heat of the last few days and of course it was how I did the majority of running in the UK. Gosh the UK - at that moment it seemed a very far off place.

And besides today was a special day not to be dampened by a bit of rain and a faulty zipper. At some point on this stage I would pass the 430 mile mark which meant that I had less than 100 miles to go. I'd long since passed the 100,000 feet of elevation so a double celebration. I'd conditioned myself not to think about the finish in Cap de Creus but now it was hard not to. It was a real possibility that I would pull it off. How would my life change?

Would it change at all? Who knows - the only certainty was that I knew deep inside that I had changed and there was no going back.

Back to the present. I'd got slight trepidation about the hotel I'd booked for this evening in Rocabruno but it was done in a hurry that morning and there was no point in worrying - que sera sera.

I actually walked a lot of the stage on the bits that I could have run - I was definitely losing my fizz but I reassured myself that I was saving myself for the final push and that it was OK to have a lay day (if running and walking 16 miles could be called a lay day).

I ambled into the town of Camprodon, the final stop for the day and after a few frantic text messages I saw Jojo in the distance. Not that you could miss her with her trade-mark bright pink shorts and matching espadrilles.

She had checked out the hotel and said that I certainly didn't have anything to worry about. We had struck gold and it was magical.

I won't do it justice but let me see if I can describe it for you. You found the entrance down a single rough track off the main road. You travelled down this for a mile crossing streams with waterfalls cascading down the rocks that aligned the track. Through lush greenery before suddenly coming cross an enormous country pile, completely isolated and with stupendous views across a valley to the mountains beyond.

How on earth had she found this Shangri-La in the heart of Catalonia when doing her recce. (It transpired that it had been a challenge and she had had to resort to phoning brother Nick at mission control in Devon who had found it on Google maps and talked her in).

The Señora was charming and made an enormous fuss of the 'famous runner'. She had an American girlfriend staying with her who worked in Hollywood and had a broken arm, complete with a large plaster cast. I know the Hollywood bit and the broken arm are a bit of a non sequitur but I'm trying to convey that this was a rather surreal cast (pun intended) for the back and beyond of the Pyrenees.

After the introductions were done and the promise of a gourmet supper for the vegetarian and a 'special pudding'

I found my room. Well, I've stayed in some hotel rooms in my time but nothing prepared me for this. The room was vast with wooden floors, rugs and antiques. There were two enormous, shuttered windows which, when pulled back, gave an uninterrupted view of the valley and mountains beyond.

After a shower in the 'antique' bathroom I sat for an hour by the window watching the sun set over the valley. By the time we met for supper I was rejuvenated.

The Hollywood friend started quizzing me on my story, but in a nice way. She was spellbound with the tales of devilry and daring (or pretended to be anyway). "Wow - so you're 60. There's a book in this you know, maybe even a film."

But before I could get carried away it was time for my 'special' supper - an omelette and salad. Next, la piece de la resistance - the pudding which I had been eagerly anticipating. But first it had to be prepared. The Señora reached into the fridge and pulled out a yoghurt pot which she turned upside down onto a plate. Next, she stretched to take a jar of strawberry jam from the cupboard and spooned a large dollop on top of the yoghurt. This was then presented to me with a fanfare and great aplomb. And do you know what it was the nicest pudding I've ever had. I mean I'm not a fan of yoghurt or supermarket jam but it's the thought that counts – there's another lesson there.

So this weary runner made his way to bed. I lay there on the enormous bed looking out through the open windows and listening to the sound of the crickets which lulled me into a long, deep sleep.

Chapter 26

Thunderbolts and lightning …

"The cave you fear to enter holds the treasures you seek"

Joseph Campbell

I woke to the sound of birdsong through the open windows and took one last look at that wonderful view before getting my act together. It was going to be another long day with another marathon thrown in for good measure and 6,000ft + of climbing. According to my faithful and by now somewhat dog-eared copy of the GR11 guide this would be the last big mountain before the Mediterranean. On the downside, it was also an area famous for massive and unpredictable thunderstorms.

I left straight from the hotel and was soon back on the GR11 and the ever familiar red, white and blue chevrons. Then I started to climb … and climb and climb. The path was well marked but it was relentless and I soon slipped into my ultra runners mantra, "one foot in front of the other, one foot in front of the other" . I tried not to stop as I knew if I gave myself any excuse then it would be stop start the whole way up which would just prolong the agony.

Instead I reflected on how my body had changed shape over the last few weeks and I cast my mind back to the dark days only four or five years back when I had been clinically obese at nearly 18 stone and was riddled with arthritis often walking with a stick. Yes, I had come a long way in more senses than one. But enough self-congratulation I wasn't there yet and although I was having one of my 'happy' days, physically I was really struggling. It was hot and humid and as usual I had run out of water and there were no alpine streams here to offer respite.

I was going to have to call on all my internal resources to get through this and I was well and truly 'red-lining'. My coping strategy was to allow myself a 30 second rest every 15 minutes and it was by using this tactic, along with some particularly blue language, that I eventually found myself at the top.

I had done it and, in theory, from here on in, it should be down hill more or less to the sea. I started the descent and passed a dilapidated monastery and a fast flowing river. Suddenly there were more people and this was to be a pattern all the way to the Mediterranean. There was a large, natural rock pool with happy kids playing and then it was another short but steep climb before the final descent.

The clouds were gathering and I knew that a storm was on the way. I also knew that I wasn't going to be able to out run it before the rendezvous. In fact I would be lucky to reach the end of the stage before night set in. Sure enough, as I started the descent, the heavens opened, this time complete with thunder and lightening.

I spotted a little refuge with a couple of adventurers sheltering in the doorway. To my amazement it was one of the climbers I had met back in Escalona who had braved the Haut Pyrenee route and with whom I had only just caught up. We swopped stories and although he suggested I should shelter because of the lightening, I decided to press on. I took a deep breath and launched myself down the mountain. The lightening was crashing right next to me as I sped down the narrow path and I've got to say it was one of the most exciting things I've ever experienced (and probably one of the more foolhardy in a long list of foolhardy exploits). But they say fortune favours the brave and all that and so it turned out to be. As night fell I saw the winking tail lights of the VW waiting patiently for me.

"Hello I've changed hotels as the one you booked was a bit grim - I hope you like it. "Oh and I've got you a pizza to keep you going until supper. You better eat it while it's hot though". "How on earth did you manage to find a hot pizza here in the middle of nowhere". "Well" she said "there's a story there …" and as I munched happily on the pizza I learned of its origins. She had found a little bar with a fridge in the corner in which she espied a pizza. Next, with virtually no Spanish and a combination of smiles and sign language, she had persuaded the owner to cook it in her own kitchen and put it in foil for the famous runner. Who said I didn't have a team to equal Kilian's and, as I've said numerous times before, this is how her world rocks.

I was very grateful for the pizza and of course the hotel was fabulous and much better than the service station style one I had chosen. It was set in a tranquil garden with a swimming pool, excellent restaurant and nice rooms too. I could hardly believe it but this was to be the final pit stop on the push to Cap de Creus.

We had tuna for supper washed down with some white Rioja as I told tall tales of the famous mountain runner running down a mountain in the pouring rain with thunderbolts and lightening crashing all around him.

Chapter 27

Ladies of the night

...

"The only thing that is ultimately real about your journey is the step that you are taking at this moment. That's all there ever is."
Alan Watts

The following morning and within minutes of leaving the hotel I was back on the GR11 and running through a shaded cork forest. I always thought of cork as being highly manufactured and I never imagined it in its natural state. I was so busy thinking of cork and all its uses that I missed treading on an Asp viper by just a few millimetres. That would have made me smart a bit and the danger switch I referred to earlier in my story was well and truly on and I became ever more vigilant. That said it was a lovely surface to run on with the cork giving a nice soft cushion to land on.

I passed a man and his dog and told them in sign language and with hisses about the snake but they looked pretty non-plussed. I think they were seasoned travellers though - the dog even had its own rucksack complete with side panniers and, as we went our separate ways, I asked if I could take a picture.

There was now a brief climb before I exited the cork forest down a wide path towards the border town of Jonqueras sprawled out below. How can I best describe Jonqueras? Well for UK readers it's a bit like Slough; for those from France imagine the back streets of Marseilles and for my Spanish friends … well imagine Jonqueras.

I approached it by running through a graffiti covered and litter strewn tunnel underneath the motorway straight into an enormous lorry park. You can imagine my surprise to see a voluptuous blonde resplendent in a bright pink and shear baby doll nightdress appear from behind a large lorry. In her left hand she clutched a rather scrawny dishevelled man who was certainly half her size and I can only assume was the owner of the truck. As she passed she gave me a broad smile and a wink, he just looked sheepish.

I made a rapid exit from the lorry park down the first street I could find where, much to my amazement were lots more scantily dressed ladies in similar attire. Perhaps it was the national dress in this part of Spain.

I beat a hasty retreat to the sound of catcalls and whistles from all sides. I was meeting Jojo in the centre of town and to this day, the best picture that has ever been taken of me, is one she took of me sprinting down Jonqueras high street like my life depended on it.

"We've got to get out of here now" I said, "I'll explain later". We piled into the car and tried to find a way out of this most interesting of towns. The trouble was it was one big set of roadworks and every time we thought we were getting out, our route was barred and we ended up back where we started. Finally we found ourselves at a T-junction with a large sign that had an arrow pointing right. "But we want to go left …. There's nothing for it we are going to have to make a 'Special Manoeuvre'."

At this juncture I should probably explain exactly what a 'Special Manoeuvre' is. Basically it is a total and flagrant disregard for all known traffic regulations and is a strictly temporary measure that should be used sparingly to extricate oneself from a situation when all else fails. So a simple version might be going the wrong way down a one way street - no point in doing three sides of a triangle - right. For a more advanced version I will site a true incident that happened to me the following year in Florence. I don't know whether you know Florence well, but it has a highly complex one way system with non essential traffic strictly barred from the city centre. I had just run across Italy and had decided to spend a couple of days in Florence to recuperate. I got completely lost and ended up driving my little Smart hire car around the famous Piazza della Signoria. Probably the only car ever to have done so and the look of terror on stall holders, Japanese tourists and the like as they scattered in all directions will shame me for ever. Having done a couple of circuits at breakneck speed I found an exit manned by two policewomen. I wound down the window and asked them the way to the parking. They were so shell shocked and dumbfounded that they duly gave me the directions open mouthed and didn't even arrest me. That would be an example of an advanced 'Special Manoeuvre' with consequences. Now you have the terminology, back to the case in hand.

"Right when I shout "Go!" aim the car for the gap in the cones and onto the other side of the road - it's our only way out." Jojo looked nervous but she is game for anything. "Go!". There was a squeal of tyres as we launched our little hire car across two lanes of traffic through the cones and onto the other side of the road that would finally take us out of Jonqueras. "Do you think tomorrow I can drop you on the outskirts". "I think that's a great idea." The journey back to the hotel was enlivened by tales of the escape from the prostitutes and the Jonqueras 'Special Manoeuvre' was not mentioned again and will be yet another entry to be saved for the memoirs.

As we returned to the hotel, storm clouds were gathering but I was determined to go for a swim so I grabbed some shorts and a towel and made my way to the pool where I joined an Italian man and his young daughter. But they were more sensible and had read the weather clouds and departed as the heavens opened accompanied by thunder and. lightening. I dived in and it was great - I love swimming in the rain although I do remember something from my school days in the dim and distant past about water and electricity ... I'm sure it will come back to me.

Chapter 28

500 miles and counting …

"The most beautiful people I've known are those who have known trials, have known struggles, have known loss, and have found their way out of the depths."

Elizabeth Kubler-Ross

I got up early, first and foremost because I had the best part of 30 miles to run today but also so that we could brave anything that the traffic system of Jonqueras threw at us.

I would pass the 500 mile mark and I might even put my hand in the Mediterranean if all went well and I was able to get as far as Llanca. Whatever happened it wouldn't be the official end though as I was determined to finish at the Cap de Creus lighthouse *a la Kilian* and then I could really say I've run from the Atlantic to the Mediterranean. But I mustn't get ahead of myself, I still had the snakes and working girls of Jonqueras to negotiate.

I was dropped on the outskirts of Jonqueras as agreed. But I didn't have a particularly auspicious start. As I got into a steady rhythm the first thing I saw was a dead snake in the road. Dead or not I gave it a wide berth and pressed on towards the coast. I hoped it wasn't an omen of some kind - me and my voodoo. I could read a message into anything if I tried hard enough.

The heat though was very real - It was already in the 30s and this was at 7.30am. My plan was to run at a slow and steady pace to try and conserve energy for the little uphill section before Llanca which I would walk. I knew in this heat that for certain I would run out of water but I knew too that there were a couple of little villages en route that were relatively well spaced out and I should be able to top up.

I was busy congratulating myself on how well organised I was this far into the trip and wasn't it amazing that I was still cognoscent and planning so well. But as is the way, I was soon brought down to earth with a bump. I had taken a wrong turn somewhere and it looked like I was skirting some kind of enormous military camp come training ground. Any minute now and the tanks would appear. I do know enough about Spain not to piss off the military or the cops and this was definitely not a case for "no point in doing three sides of the triangle - right".

I slunk off as fast as I could, re-tracing my steps and sure enough I came to a huge sign "Attencion - Zona Militar!" how on earth had I managed to miss that. I took a selfie to make sure I was still there and when I look back on it now I can see how tired I was and that I was definitely running on empty. As the saying goes "all the lights are on but no one is at home".

I was starting to feel very disorientated and got the phone out to check that I was heading in the right direction. I've had this feeling at the end of very long ultras - you really do start hallucinating and imagining all kinds of weird and wonderful things, normally involving animals in my case. Cows singing and dancing, badgers leaping over horse jumps - that kind of thing, all quite normal. I took the last swig of water, pulled myself up straight and on I went. I passed a little village which had a bar again with the obligatory Señora and dog (was it the same one each time) and I filled up with water and had a coffee to try and 'sober up' and get my act together.

Through the village of Vilamaniscle where there was a really nice hotel with a bar and swimming pool and a charming waiter who happily took my order for ice cream, water, Aquarius and coffee despite my ragged and dishevelled appearance. Finally, finally finally I started the rocky climb that would allow me to look down on Llanca and the Mediterranean.

There were a couple of Forest Rangers who I think were checking for fires - it was as dry as tinder here and then, there it was - the Mediterranean and what this quest had been all about. It was beautiful, a turquoise blue, exactly as you would imagine the Mediterranean to be and very different from the Atlantic which I had dipped my hand in a few weeks before. It was a long trek to Llanca and the final few miles seemed to take forever. But eventually I got to the arranged rendezvous on the seafront and just slumped against a wall by the side of the beach. The quartermaster was there with ice creams, carbs in the form of cheese sandwiches and of course Aquarius by the litre. "One more day, one more day" was the mantra going through my mind as I stared into the horizon.

When I had recovered we made our way down to the port and the car and I regaled Jojo with tales of snakes and dehydration and how I took on the might of Spain's army single handedly.

As we made our way back to the hotel my eyes closed and I kept repeating the mantra to myself "one more day, one more day".

Chapter 29

"Old Kilian" …

"The hero journey is inside of you; tear off the veils and open the mystery of yourself."
Joseph Campbell

I was quiet in the car on the way to Llanca and the drop off point.

It's not that I was depressed about this being the last day - I don't really show too many emotions for reasons I've already alluded to. No, I was flash-backing (in a good way) the events of the last four weeks - a kaleidoscope of colours, sounds, smells, shapes, scenery, friendly people and friendly dogs (for the most part). The challenges too - oh yes there had been plenty of obstacles put in my path, from lack of food, dehydration, getting lost, perpendicular drops, ice walls and dark tunnels to name but a few. And despite the immortal words of my father who, when we thanked him for taking us somewhere, would retort "we're not there yet" I allowed myself to reflect a little bit on how I'd changed.

It's hard to describe, but if I was asked to name one thing, I would say that for the first time in my life since leaving Africa at the age of six, I had found some quiet inner confidence and self esteem. The emphasis being on the word "quiet". I didn't have to prove to anyone that I existed, or that I was kind, or clever or that I deserved to be noticed.

I had also proved to myself that you can do just about anything in life if you are determined enough and you don't have to be a complete shit either, contrary to popular opinion.

I had overcome debilitating Arthritis, CPTSD, Aspergers, obesity, chronic people-pleasing tendencies and a whole range of injuries and ailments including, but not limited to, a herniated disc, achilles tendinitis, hypertension and insomnia. What's more I had overcome these challenges, for the most part myself. Although I recognised that I was incredibly fortunate to have the support of my wife and family who had backed me every step of the way.

I was on the threshold of doing something truly remarkable. I wasn't a 'Kilian' – just a very ordinary person doing something extraordinary.

So probably that's the reason I was quiet on the drive to Llanca this particular Sunday morning.

But enough soul searching and introspection. You want to know what happened on that final, fateful day – right?

Jojo treated me to breakfast at a lovely café in the centre. She was busy telling the long suffering waiter all about my adventure. "Muy bien - let me know how you get on this evening, I'll still be working". Llanca was in party mood with lots of market stalls and entertainment being set up. There would be plenty of time for that tonight - hopefully.

But first I had one final job to do. I strapped on my runner's vest for the final time this trip and headed away from the milieu towards the GR11 and Cap de Creus just

17 miles away.

I crossed a deserted car park and within minutes I was back on the GR11 and up and up a narrow switchback path. The heat was intense and already I was having to take in copious amounts of water. I just knew it - I had been proved right and today was going to have a nasty sting in the tail.

I met a couple coming down the path and we said our "Holas". They were from Barcelona and were keen to practice their perfect English. "Are you on your Sunday jog" they asked. "Something like that" I replied. We said our goodbyes and I trudged on more like a climber making the final steps up Everest than a mountain trail runner.

The next excitement was a group of trail runners who were out for their Sunday practice. They came whooping and hollering past me as I pressed myself to the side of the path. "Hola, hola, hola". And then they were gone.

I finally got to the top and made the descent to the aptly named Mars which was the last bit of civilisation before the volcanic crop and the lighthouse. Ever closer, ever closer, just miles away now. In Mars I bought an ice cream, a big bottle of water and an Aquarius. I proffered a 50 euro note and for one terrible moment I thought the shopkeeper wasn't going to accept it. We compromised by me having two of everything and I continued on my weary way.

Mars had everything including two policemen diligently patrolling the beach until they moved away and I saw a sign "NUDIST BEACH". Some things never change.

Next, down a really scruffy bit of scrubland where to my amazement I followed an old van crawling along the path over the rocks and potholes. And I thought my sense of direction was bad.

I kept going with sweat pouring down my face blackened by dirt and volcanic dust, all hope of staying moderately hydrated abandoned.

"Come on you can do it, you can do it" I passed another old monastery (they always pick remote places don't they - maybe it's a kind of penance?) before a small ascent onto the volcanic rock. And then the sign "Cap de Creus lighthouse". I took a picture for posterity and realised that tears were mixed with the sweat and grime. "That's funny I don't 'do' emotion" I thought to myself.

The rock was treacherous and it was so easy to trip as, needless to say, I had strayed off the path. But I could see the lighthouse and it was getting closer and closer.

And so it was, that at 5:53pm on a beautiful yet windy Sunday afternoon, I climbed a short ramp to take me to the Cap de Creus lighthouse. Five hundred and twenty seven miles, 120,000ft + of ascent and 27 days from setting out from Cap d'Higier and the Atlantic Ocean.

"You've done it, you've done it, you've done it" squawked Jojo who was patiently waiting at the top of the ramp struggling to hold onto some balloons in the howling wind. "Have you got anything to eat" I replied.

Somehow she had got hold of the balloons and made friends with the lady in the tourist office who stored them there much to their joint amusement. I did a little photo call with the balloons and Jojo wanted to know how I felt. "Well I'm quite hungry - shall we go back to where we had breakfast and see our waiter friend?" She knew me well enough to know this was all she was going to get and we hopped in the car and headed back to Llanca.

You will be delighted to know that we did get lost on the way back to Llanca which is quite difficult to do on a single track road. But we did manage to find our restaurant and our waiter who was still on duty. I ordered a huge beer (my" Ice Cold In Alex" moment for those of you who've seen the classic film - and if you haven't go and find it!)

"Hola, you did it then" said the waiter as he brought my beer … he stopped a few moments to have a think … "I shall call you 'old Kilian'".

I smiled as I took a sip of beer - I might not have found Kilian but I had found myself and maybe that wasn't such a bad substitute.

Printed in Great Britain
by Amazon